CHINA

for Businesswomen

CHINA

for Businesswomen

A Strategic Guide to Travel, Negotiating, and Cultural Differences

Tracey Wilen-Daugenti

With contributions by Yuen Yuen Ang,
Pamela Galley, and Patricia D. Wilen

Stone Bridge Press • Berkeley, California

Published by
Stone Bridge Press
P. O. Box 8208
Berkeley, CA 94707
TEL 510-524-8732 • sbp@stonebridge.com • www.stonebridge.com

NOTE TO READERS: Regulations, procedures, addresses, and phone numbers change frequently. Information contained in this book was believed to be correct at the time of publication. Neither the author nor the publisher can be responsible for any loss or damage from the use or misuse of information contained in this book. Please send corrections and updates for future editions to sbp@stonebridge.com.

Printed in the United States of America.

2011 2010 2009 2008 2007   10 9 8 7 6 5 4 3 2 1

LIBRARY OF CONGRESS CATALOGING-IN-PUBLICATION DATA

Wilen-Daugenti, Tracey.
  China for businesswomen: a strategic guide to travel, negotiating, and cultural differences / Tracey Wilen-Daugenti.
      p. cm.
  Includes bibliographical references.
  ISBN-13: 978-1-933330-28-0 (pbk.)

  1. China—Commerce—Handbooks, manuals, etc. 2. Businesswomen—Handbooks, manuals, etc.   I. Title.
  HF3837.W55 2007
  395.5'20820951—dc22
                                2007035585

CONTENTS

ACKNOWLEDGMENTS

I would like to thank the many women who have supported this book effort through their participation in interviews. Of particular value was their advice regarding strategies and best practices, and their sharing of experiences so that women can continue to advance and excel in business.

My special thanks go to to the key contributors: Patricia Wilen, Ph.D. and Yuen Yuen Ang have enhanced the content of the book with their unique expertise and experiences. Thank you to Pamela Galley, RN for her contribution on health in China, and to Suresh Vege for research data and analysis. I would also like to express my gratitude to the travel, airline, and hospitality experts I have met through my numerous business trips and who are every day instrumental in helping us to safely conduct business around the globe.

Dr. Tracey Wilen-Daugenti

# INTRODUCTION

Why China?

Globalization has swept China. Tremendous transformations have taken place over the past thirty years as the country has moved from Communism to a modern and global market economy. As China becomes the world's ultimate business destination, companies from the United States and virtually everywhere else are clamoring to claim a stake in the Chinese market.

Pick up a newspaper or magazine anywhere and much of the talk today is about China—the fastest-growing and sixth-largest economy in the world. The Chinese economy has grown at an annual rate of 10 percent in the past fifteen years, by far the world's highest growth rate. In 2004 its $1.65 trillion economy was about one-seventh the size of the U.S. economy. Thirty years ago when Nixon first visited, China was an economic backwater in terms of international trade; today China is a major partner and competitor with the United States in production, exports, and entrepreneurship.

China is the world's largest producer of manufactured goods, making 40 percent of all American furniture and 70 percent of the world's toys. Its cheaply produced clothing is pushing out other manufacturers in the developed world. The United States is one of China's primary suppliers of power-generating equipment, aircraft and parts, computers and industrial machinery, raw materials, chemicals, and agricultural products. China had a trade surplus with the U.S. of $162 billion in 2004.

In 2003 exports and imports by foreign companies operating in China rose by 40 percent. China's total trade in 2004 surpassed $1.1 trillion, making China the world's third-largest trading nation after the U.S. and Germany, pushing Japan into fourth place. Some predict that China will one day become the world's largest trading nation.

With its accession to the World Trade Organization (WTO) in December 2001, China agreed to lower tariffs and abolish market barriers. This far-reaching trade liberalization agreement will speed up China's integration into the global economy. Furthermore, China will host the Olympics in Beijing City in 2008, drawing more global attention to its business and travel opportunities.

The growing importance of international trade and commerce with China has created a great demand for cross-cultural preparation among Western corporations. Working in a vastly different culture like China requires social skills that go beyond expertise in technical areas like finance or software programming. It also requires knowledge of the Chinese culture, its protocols, beliefs, and business style.

CROSS-CULTURAL PREPARATION

Research conducted on the successes and failures of employees who have relocated to another country to conduct business found that of fifty-one American companies, only 12 percent offered any cross-cultural training.[1] Even when formal training is provided by the firm, it is mostly inadequate. Expatriates can try to educate themselves by reading travel guidebooks or taking language classes at a local college, but many employees who conduct business outside of the home country find themselves frustrated and lost.

As I have highlighted in my book *Basic Guide for Women in International Business*, American firms often place personnel in a foreign culture with the incorrect expectation that interactions there will mirror those in the U.S. As a result, although American businesspeople who travel to China hope to make a good impression, they often do not. Actions that may be considered appropriate for professionals in corporate America may be perceived as arrogant, insensitive, or aggressive in China. Cultural misunderstandings can jeopardize business success.

Business researchers have found a strong relationship between the rigor of selection and training procedures and an expatriate's ability to perform successfully in a foreign environment. Advance cultural preparation—learning about the beliefs, norms, and protocol of a foreign environment—is a must for effective international business.

WOMEN ON THE GO

In an increasingly globalized international economy, more American businesspeople are traveling abroad than ever before. While in the past only senior executives traveled overseas, today business travelers represent many organizational levels and areas of functional expertise.

In particular, more and more businesswomen are now on the go. The U.S. Department of Travel reports that women now account for over 40 percent of international business travel and over 55 percent of domestic travel. As one senior HR executive remarked, "In high-tech industries, there is no time for discrimination. If you breathe and can do the job, you will go overseas on business."

Therefore, a new type of cosmopolitan, multilingual, versatile executive who functions effectively across national borders is now in demand. Companies are beginning to focus less on an employee's gender but more on who best succeeds internationally. Increasingly, firms are using cross-cultural skills as a basis for deciding whom to send on foreign assignments.

As American firms expand their operations to China, more female executives and entrepreneurs are traveling to China for business. Over one million Americans visit China each year. This is no wonder as China is an attractive market for American companies, many of which are run by women.

According to the Small Business Administration, from 1987 to 1997, the number of women-owned businesses increased 89 percent to an estimated 8.5 million. As of 1999, women-owned firms accounted for 38 percent of all firms and 55 percent of startups in the United States. Women-owned businesses generated $3.1 trillion in revenue, an increase of 209 percent between 1987 and 1997.[2] More than one in eighteen adult women in the U.S. is a business owner. Nearly 6 percent of all adult women now own and run businesses and contribute substantially to the nation's economy.[3]

About This Book

Based on interviews with women executives and entrepreneurs who have conducted business in China, this book outlines strategies to help women achieve business success internationally. *China for Businesswomen* focuses on strategies for women who conduct or plan to conduct business in China. These women come from a variety of industries (retail, high technology, manufacturing, services, government, tourism, and more), countries (U.S., Canada, Europe, and East Asia), and positions (CEO, partners, mid-level managers, entrepreneurs).

Besides the organizational hurdles encountered back home, American businesswomen will face additional gender barriers in China. Women are usually left to fend for themselves and have few sources to turn to for advice. Even existing business guidebooks on China can be misleading. Most books in this genre are written by men and for men. They generally do not address issues particular to women in international business. Worse, they sometimes suggest that women should not even be sent on overseas business trips because of presumably insurmountable gender biases in China.

In contrast, my own research over the years has found that women can be successful in international business.

This book presents you with valuable experiences and advice for avoiding cultural traps and achieving business success in China. Section One presents practical information on traveling in China, which first-time travelers will find particularly helpful. Section Two focuses on several key aspects of doing business in China, with a unique focus on gender issues, and Section Three illuminates the history and evolution of Chinese gender norms.

Crucial strategies you will learn in this book include:

- Establishing credibility and being prepared before you go
- Gaining cultural awareness of gender perceptions in the West versus China
- Understanding the protocol and processes of negotiation in China
- Coping with gender discrimination and harassment
- Learning about wining, dining, and gift-making protocol

For a democratic, capitalist society like the United States, it is a great challenge to understand and work in a vastly different culture like China, especially for foreign women. As Madame Xie Heng, a prominent Chinese author and diplomat, noted, "China is both a very old country and a very new country at once, and its attitudes toward women reflect that duality."[4] I do believe that we can begin to clear cultural hurdles by making a conscious effort at cross-cultural understanding and preparation. I hope this book can serve as a useful guide for all businesswomen (and perhaps even businessmen!) as you venture into the Chinese market.

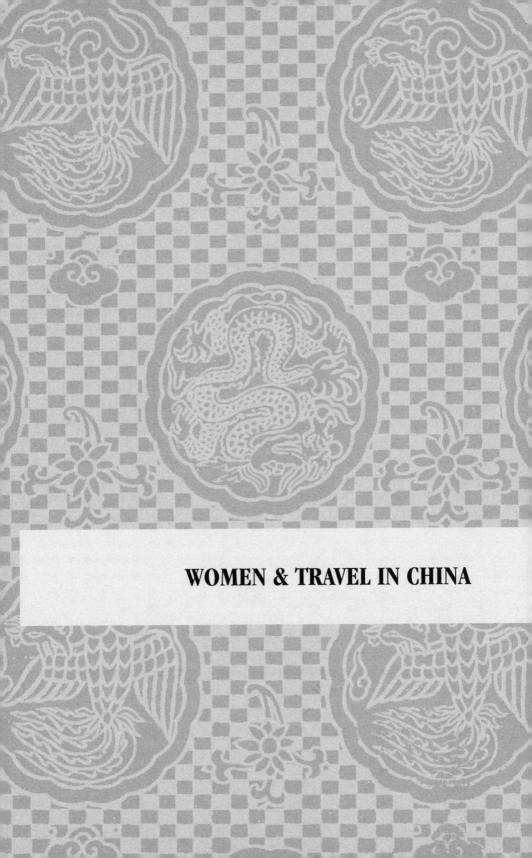

WOMEN & TRAVEL IN CHINA

1

BEFORE YOU GO

Preparing for Your Business Meeting

MAKING CONTACTS

Many cultures outside of the U.S. thrive on personal and informal relationships. The Chinese prefer to work with people with whom they are already familiar. Thus, a cold call is not an advisable approach to meeting people in China; it is highly unlikely to elicit a positive response. Instead, if you know someone who is close to the firm that you desire to contact, try to meet your counterparts with the help of this connection. Working through an organization that can acquaint you with an initial contact is ideal. Many of these third-party firms are industry-related and advertise frequently in local trade magazines. Other venues through which you can meet potential contacts and clients include conferences and trade shows; many are held in the U.S. You should target a local trade conference for the specific region of China where you would like to make contacts.

Entrepreneurs and large firms should take advantage of the resources offered to U.S. firms by the Department of Commerce (www.ita.doc.gov). A trade mission is particularly valuable for small firms that do not have a presence in China, and is usually organized by your local department of commerce. To increase the visibility of the group, trade missions are headed by notable figures, such as the mayor of your city or the business leader of a major organization. The cost of trade missions usually ranges from $2,000 to $5,000 and includes hotel, flight, and appointment charges. The Department of Commerce also offers a great deal of expert advice, either free or for a nominal fee, to assist you in creating a business plan or in developing export opportunities.

> ### Take Advantage of the Commerce Department
>
> "Take advantage of the Commerce Department. Here in Europe our Commerce Minister, who organizes several missions to China, watches the Chinese market carefully. They try to get companies and political officials to go on such trips. [The commerce department] is very aggressive in the China market. They pay all the expenses for the trips organized to sign deals. In the U.S., you have department trade missions and support that is low cost and effective for small and medium business owners."
> (Washington, D.C.)

Once you have obtained business cards and made contacts, follow up with a letter thanking these people for their time. Alternatively, you could send a short e-mail to remind your contact of the acquaintance made, and then follow up with a letter and press kit that explains your firm, products, and services. You could also include videos or CDs to help your customers visualize and understand your business. If you are planning to visit your potential business partners, request an appointment by letter or fax. Be specific in what you intend to discuss, who the participants are from your firm, and provide a few suggested dates. Then allow time for response to your request. Try to make these arrangements at least three weeks before you travel. You may need this much time to book hotels and flights.

RESEARCHING THE FIRM

To be effective in international business you must conduct thorough research on the company of interest. Many firms in China now have Web sites, so you should visit them as part of your preparation. A big firm like Haier, a Chinese appliance company with operations in the U.S., boasts an English–Chinese Web site. In addition, you can consult reputable commercial firms, such as Dun and Bradstreet (www.dnb.com), for credit and various other reports. If the firm is large, there is a good chance something will be in the files. If the firm has filed with the Securities and Exchange Commission (SEC), you can access information at www.edgar.com.

Of course, if the firm is small and does not have a U.S. office, gathering information becomes more difficult. Many companies outside of the U.S. are not required to file reports, as American firms do. For a start, you can visit www.tradeport. org, which offers basic information on key exports, current economic situation, etc., compiled by the U.S. Department of Commerce. If you can locate the Chinese-language Web site of the company you are planning to visit, it would pay to have the information translated. If the company is listed on major Asian stock markets, financial information can be found in the *China Stock Directory*, an English-language guide to Chinese companies listed in China, Singapore, Hong Kong, London, the U.S., and Tokyo.[5] Try to talk to people who have worked with the companies you are contacting to get an idea of how they conduct business, their reputation, management structure, and so on.

CREATING AN AGENDA

Once you have made an appointment to meet with business-people in China, you should propose an agenda specifying what issues are to be discussed at the meeting. Many American businesswomen have discovered that sending an agenda in advance helps establish your position as a leader of your group.

An effective agenda includes a statement of purpose as well as a list of participants and their positions in your company. List your team members according to their rank. If you are providing the agenda, make sure to include your name and title prominently. For women in particular, this helps to state in writing that you will be leading the business meeting. Make sure your rank and title are aligned with that of your Chinese counterpart.

Networking

"U.S. firms frequently forget that business is not conducted in a direct manner all over the world. For example, in China it is very important to establish relationships and have a network of people you know in order to get business done. There were some executives in my firm who were bidding for projects in China. They arrived jetlagged from the trip, made no effort to establish rapport, learn about the culture, or even learn a word of Mandarin. It was no wonder that we did not win the bid."
(Shanghai, China)

When in China the actual meeting may not follow your proposed agenda. Oftentimes, issues you had not expected but that are important to the Chinese may arise, and the discussion can go off on a different track. Nevertheless, proposing an agenda can help set the direction of the meeting and initiate constructive dialogue. To avoid surprises, allow your counterparts sufficient time to review your agenda and provide comments.

BUSINESS CARDS

Business cards are very important in China. The information on the card helps identify who you are and your position in the firm. For women, this can help enhance credibility by indicating your status in the firm's hierarchy. Make sure you use a title that is well understood cross-culturally, for example, "manager" or "director." A title like "specialist" may cause confusion. Many women advise that you may need to inflate your title to ensure that an appropriate representative will be sent to meet with you. The Chinese will usually match rank for rank. Having a more important sounding title, for example, "manager" rather than "senior administrator," can help you gain more respect.

Most business cards are translated into Mandarin on the reverse side. If you have your business cards translated before you go to China, make sure you choose a reputable translation firm, and then, if possible, have the cards proofread by a native Chinese speaker. Translation errors can cause much embarrassment, so it is important to double-check. Some businesswomen also suggest using a Chinese name so that your name can be easily pronounced and remembered. Most English names can be phonetically translated into Chinese. For example, Jenny could be Zhenni and Katie could be Kaidi. The most common way to format your cards in China is to have your name and title printed in Chinese characters vertically from top to bottom, right to left on the back of the card. Make sure your printer is knowledgeable about card conventions and formats.

Some travelers prefer having their cards translated when they arrive in China. Many hotels have a business card translation service or can recommend a local firm. Some can translate and print cards in twenty-four hours, while others may take a few days. Plan to bring more business cards with you because meetings in China are usually attended by many participants.

LEARNING CONVERSATIONAL MANDARIN

Language is the window into every culture. If you plan on doing long-term business in China, it definitely pays to learn some Mandarin. Speaking some Mandarin or at least understanding basic conversation can help you get around airports and hotels, order food, ask for help, and build rapport with the locals. It will come in useful during meetings and negotiations, especially if your counterparts are not fluent in English. When you socialize with the Chinese and speak some Mandarin, it shows them that you are committed to learning the culture and establishing your business in China.

If you are pressed for time, the best option for learning Mandarin would be to hire a private tutor who can accommodate your schedule. Your private tutor may also offer useful advice in navigating the local culture, checking translations, or even suggesting business resources. You can find a private tutor by searching community classifieds or posting an advertisement at the nearest university, where a lecturer or graduate student might be interested in providing such services. Web sites like www.zapchinese.com provide free online Mandarin lessons and a list of private tutors in the U.S.

Traveling to Your Business Destination

GATHERING INFORMATION

Before you go, visit the English-language Web site of the China National Tourist Office (www.cnto.org), which has branch offices in Los Angeles and New York. You can contact these offices for more information on travel issues, such as customs clearance and health requirements. In addition, major automobile clubs such as AAA have touring books and maps for their members.

Upon arrival in China, you'll find that most hotels offer an English-speaking local guide and maps of the city you are visiting. You can usually get a local newspaper on the airplane to read up on the country, events, and local events. Usually one of the local TV news stations offered by hotels broadcasts in English.

PASSPORTS AND VISAS

Travel to China requires a passport. If you do not have a passport, make sure you allow yourself plenty of time to get one. You can find a passport center in your local phone book or by searching for passport applications on the World Wide Web. If you already have a passport, make sure it will not expire during the trip. Be aware that some countries require that your passport be valid up to six months from the start date of your trip. For current information on how to get a passport and what you need for overseas travel, go to travel.state.gov/passport_services.html.

In addition to a passport, travel to China requires a visa. Visas allow you entry into a country for a specific period of time; they need to be renewed for continued visits. If you are not sure of the requirements, check with the Chinese embassy in your area. Make sure you procure enough photos for your passport and visas. To apply for a visa for travel to China, you will need two passport-size photos. If you plan to travel in and out of the country several times during the course of your visit, be sure to get a visa allowing multiple visits. For current visa information go to travel.state.gov/foreignentryreqs.html.

HEALTH ISSUES

It is important to check in advance what immunization shots are required for travel to China. For most travel, doctors will provide you a yellow card for your passport that you should keep, as some shots last ten years while others last only three or four. For more information you can call the International Travelers' Hotline at the Centers for Disease Control and Prevention at (404) 332-4559 or visit their Web site at www.cdc. gov/travel. Check with your company to see what medical coverage you have for overseas travel. Some companies may have an overseas medical hotline, while others may have specific hospitals or travel doctors with which they network. For more information on health and immunization issues when traveling, refer to Chapter 3, "Health Issues When Traveling."

BOOKING FLIGHTS

Check flight availability, times, and rates to the cities you plan to visit in China well in advance of your trip. Make sure that your travel does not conflict with major holidays (see later in this chapter) or events. Airline travel to China's key business cities is very crowded and many flights are oversold. You may pay a premium to fly there or have to wait. A travel agent can help you with flight alternatives, hotel bookings, travel routes, and advance notice of special rates on commonly traveled flight paths.

- Check the flight arrival date and time to be sure you have sufficient time to arrive at your meetings. It is easy to make mistakes when traveling across time zones. You will lose a day in your travel to China and gain it back on the return.
- Some travelers advise arriving the day before the business meeting in order to adjust to time zone changes.
- Make sure you reconfirm your flight twenty-four hours in advance. Flight times change frequently, and passengers are not always notified. Your hotel desk clerk or concierge will usually assist with this.
- Airport construction fees in China amount to 90 yuan (US$11) for international flights, 50 yuan (about US$6) for domestic flights, and 10 yuan for branch flight routes. Since September 1, 2004, the airport construction fee has

been included in the airfare, which is listed in the tax item on the ticket. Those who are passing through an airport onto other destinations are exempt.

BOOKING HOTELS

Book your hotel well in advance, as hotel rooms fill up quickly with business travelers and tourists; do not wait until you arrive to find a hotel. Choose a hotel close to your meeting place, since many cities in China are heavily congested and require extra travel time. For safety reasons, stay in a major hotel in a populated area. When you travel to a Chinese city, you will find Western hotel chains and those that are government owned. Women interviewed have preferred the former as they offer more services and are more familiar. If you are on your first trip, consider staying in a Western hotel though it could be more expensive.

- Dry-cleaning services are generally available in four- or five-star hotels. Consider using them if you are on a long trip and need to pack efficiently. Check with the hotel on the pick-up and return time. In some modern hotels there are now 24-hour dry cleaning services offering turnaround within hours, but in others, it may take up to two days.
- Many hotels in China offer massages, spa services, manicures, and other amenities welcomed by business travelers at relatively affordable prices.
- Many hotels also have swimming pools that are heated, so plan to bring a suit to enjoy a swim during your stay.

BOOKING CAR SERVICES

Most businesspeople have found that it is well worth the money to arrange a car service during your stay in China. This can be easily arranged by your travel agent or through tour offices, ho-

tels, airlines, or corporate travel. The cost is relatively low and the driver will stay with you for business meetings, dinners, and even sightseeing. Many suggest hiring a driver who can speak some English and who can also serve as a city guide. Some host firms will arrange car services for you. If you do not have a car arranged, you should check whether your hotel offers a shuttle or limo service to your hotel when you arrive. The service is more expensive but well worth it if you are arriving late and do not wish to bargain with taxi drivers.

Taxi services have improved tremendously in big cities like Shanghai and Beijing, in anticipation of major events like the Olympics in 2008 in Beijing and Expo in Shanghai in 2010. However, do not expect the same level of service in other cities. As most drivers do not speak English fluently or at all, make sure you have the address of where you are going in Chinese, and better still, a map. If all else fails, call the hotel concierge from the car and give the phone to the driver for directions to your location.

LUGGAGE

For many businesswomen, travel to China means moving between several cities or regions. For some this may mean flying a few times during a given week with short stays. Most businesswomen agree that packing light is essential for business travel; you will save on packing time and will more likely avoid a customs check at the airport. Many airports will check the size and number of bags you are carrying for intercity flights and will check your luggage if it is too big or if you have too many items.

Bring luggage that is not too bulky; luggage on wheels is very helpful. Stick to carry-on luggage if possible. Baggage delay or loss is not uncommon in China, and you and your group can waste a lot of time reporting the problem. If you do have to check your bags, make sure to pack a change of clothing and some toiletries in a carry-on bag in case your luggage gets lost.

For some business executives, travel to China may mean spending several weeks in one location before moving on to the next stop. To keep luggage minimal, pack enough variations in your wardrobe to keep your outfits fresh. Plan to hand wash and use dry cleaning services during your trip.

GENERAL PACKING TIPS

- To lighten your travel load, consider making a list, outlining in detail what you need, what you can discard along the way, and what you do not need to carry. For example, four- and five-star hotels usually provide a hair dryer, shampoo, and soap.

> ### *Hiring a Personal Driver*
> "I hired a guide for the whole trip to pick us up, take us to meetings, and tour the city. We had a driver the whole time. He showed us so much of China that we would not have seen. I learned from him that eight is a lucky number. We arranged for a guide because we did not speak the language. It was very inexpensive and we arranged it through a business travel service, such as American Express. I told him that I wanted to see more than the tourist spots and to see how people actually live. (Cambridge, Massachusetts)

- Stick to conservative color schemes, such as gray, navy, black, olive, and brown. Try to have your clothes blend with one another so you can interchange them. It is best to avoid loud colors.
- Pack dark, versatile clothes that don't wrinkle and can be easily layered. Clothing will wrinkle if it is loosely packed. Factor this in when you are choosing a travel bag. Many women are using soft roller duffel bags on wheels that are smaller, lighter, and can fit more items easily.
- Many business executives roll their clothes to create more packing room and hang them when they arrive. You can

also layer your clothes with dry cleaning plastic bags, or hang them in a garment bag. This will help the clothes slide against each other and not wrinkle. If your clothes are wrinkled you can steam them in the bathroom. Turn the shower on and close the tub drain so it holds water. Run the shower at its hottest temperature until the bathroom is steamy. Turn the shower off, close the door and leave the clothes hanging in the steam. You may find a travel steamer is a particularly worthwhile investment; they are very small and light, fairly inexpensive, and a surer bet to get those wrinkles out (but don't forget an adapter).

- If you are flying, put your toiletries in ziplock plastic bags to guard against leaks caused by pressure.

- If you have reading to do, consider making copies so that you can discard the materials along the way. If you have magazines, rip out or copy the articles of interest and leave the rest behind.

- Bring an adapter kit (or more, depending on usage needs), which you will need for your computer, cell phone, hair dryer, and other electronics. You can find these in most electronics and travel stores, and occasionally in airline in-flight catalogues. In some hotels you may be able to borrow adapters, but don't count on it.

- In cool, wet winter areas, wool suits, jackets, and dresses are best, since wool soaks up moisture while keeping you warm. A light jacket or cardigan sweater is usually a good item to bring anywhere. For hot, humid areas, linen and cotton suits are most comfortable.

- For rainy seasons, bring a raincoat and a folding umbrella. (Some business hotels also offer umbrellas for use by their guests.)

- If you are moving through temperature zones, plan to layer your clothes so that you can make the most use of your outfits.

- Bring sample sizes of products that you use such as perfumes, hair and face products, so that you can travel light. Pack toiletry items that might come in handy such as tissues and antiseptic wipes.
- Eliminate bulky items such as pill bottles by putting what you need for your trip into a small zip bag or case.
- Limit the pairs of shoes you pack, as they tend to take up room. If you can, bring one pair that can work with a variety of outfits and temperatures and one that is comfortable for sightseeing and shopping. Pack things in your shoes to maximize space, such as underwear, socks, or loose items.

PACKING FOR A WEEK

For an average business trip of one week, most women agree that one jacket with a few coordinating skirts or slacks and several varied blouses should suffice. If your trip extends to two weeks, then you may want to add an extra blazer and an additional skirt or pair of slacks. You can dry clean at the hotels at a relatively low cost, and many offer overnight or hourly services. Combinations of black and white (solids and patterns) or brown and tan tones are popular among businesswomen, as they are easy to coordinate with many colors of tops. Good walking shoes are essential to manage the cobblestones, rough construction areas and train stations, as well as inclement weather. A computer bag can serve as a handbag if needed. Pack minimal makeup and jewelry.

CHOOSING AND PACKING ATTIRE

When attending meetings in China, plan to dress conservatively as you would in American business meetings. The Chinese associate your attire with the business stature of your firm. Dark or plain suits are safe options. Skirts and pants are both fine. Dresses are generally not worn unless covered by a jacket. Avoid bright eye shadow, dangling earrings, and bangle bracelets. Wear hosiery in subtle natural shades. Avoid tights, bright fashion colors and designs, though you can match colored shirts with a dark suit. Wear low-heeled, closed-toe, business shoes. In short: exercise good taste. As with cosmopolitan areas around the globe, Chinese women in the big cities dress very fashionably. So while you should dress appropriately, you would not wish to appear underdressed for social occasions. You should also pack some informal clothing for sightseeing excursions.

Cities in China vary in climate, and depending on the season, it can range from extremely cold to extremely hot. You may need to pack for multiple temperature zones if you are moving from city to city. It is generally not advisable for women to wear low-cut blouses or camisoles, even in the warmest climates, as they can draw undesirable attention. Find out the temperature and weather conditions for the city you plan to visit before packing.

Spring and fall are the most desirable times to visit Shanghai, which is milder than Beijing. Summers can be very hot, and the coldest period is January and February (it rarely snows). Late August to September is typhoon season and there can be quite a lot of rain. A suit blazer should suffice in the spring and summer, add an overcoat in the fall and winter. Layer with short- and long-sleeved shirts and sweaters to manage the weather day to day.

Beijing summers are very warm, particularly in July, and the winter can be especially cold in January. There are frequent sandstorms in the spring (from the Gobi Desert). The best time to visit is September and October. Spring is the rainy season, and there are generally showers in the summer and fall as well, so pack a portable umbrella. If you are planning to squeeze in some sightseeing in the fall or winter, bring warm clothes, including a hat, gloves, and an umbrella for visiting outdoor sites such as Tiananmen Square, the Forbidden City, and the Great Wall, which can get exceptionally cold.

PACKING PERSONAL AMENITIES

When you are traveling in China, you will find that most hotels and high-end restaurants have flush toilets. Once you are out in the suburbs or rural areas, however, you may find only "squat toilets." These are basically troughs in the floor, with or without a ceramic fitting, over which you must squat. Often there is one flush toilet in the row at the end, so it's a good idea to do a quick check. Carry pocket-sized tissue packets with you since toilet paper is usually not offered. Bring along antiseptic toilettes to wash your hands, as there won't be paper towels.

Bring personal sanitary items with you from home. Depending on where you are traveling (major cities are fine), you may not find the kind you need, especially in more rural areas. Hotels in China generally offer basic amenities in the room, such as shampoo, toothbrush and toothpaste, slippers and robes, shower cap, etc. Many hotels will provide a list of what they have in stock if you have forgotten something.

Useful Information for Travelers

CURRENCY

To avoid airport lines, some travelers prefer to exchange currency before boarding their international flight. Others wait until they arrive and exchange money at one of the local bank stalls at the airport. You can acquire currency at your local bank before you travel for better exchange rates. Many airports have ATMs (Automatic Teller Machines) on site. Most travelers prefer to use ATMs as they offer the best currency exchange rates with the lowest administration fees. ATMs are only found in the major cities.

Chinese money is called Renminbi (RMB), which means "The People's Currency." The popular unit of RMB is yuan. The official exchange rate between U.S. dollar and Renminbi yuan currently is about 1:7.5 (1 dollar = 7.5 yuan). For up-to-date exchange rates, you can refer to www.xe.com. One yuan equals 10 jiao, 1 jiao equals 10 fen. In some parts of China the yuan is known as kuai and jiao is mao. Chinese currency is issued in the following denominations: one, two, five, ten, twenty, fifty, and one hundred yuan; one, two, and five jiao; and one, two, and five fen.

- Use the ATM to get cash when you are in China for the best exchange rate. ATMs are now popular in major cities, offer a current exchange rate, and charge a minor transaction fee. They usually offer better rates than hotels. Make sure you use an ATM that is in a safe, populated location such as the airport or a major shopping center.
- Credit cards are generally accepted in major cities and hotels. Don't be surprised if you find places that only accept cash.

THE 24-HOUR CLOCK

Most countries outside of the U.S. use the 24-hour clock, more commonly known to many Americans as military time. The day is divided into twenty-four hours instead of twelve, running from midnight (00:00) to midnight (24:00). Morning times are readily identifiable, but afternoon and evening hours become a little trickier to read, for example, 1 P.M. becomes 1300 hours. Slight mistakes reading the time can lead to missed meetings and flights, and can happen very easily, especially in the fog of jet lag, so be sure to double-check your conversions. An easy way to convert the time back to the U.S. clock is to subtract 12, so 1800 hours would be 18 minus 12, or 6 P.M.

TEMPERATURE CONVERSION

To convert a Fahrenheit temperature to the Celsius (or Centigrade) scale, subtract 32 and then divide by 1.8. To convert Celsius into Fahrenheit, multiply the Celsius temperature by 1.8, and then add 32. An easier way to make approximate conversions is to subtract 30 from Fahrenheit and divide by 2 to get Celsius; for Fahrenheit, double the Celsius temperature and add 30.

Units of Length [6]

1 kilometer = 2 li = 0.62 miles
1 meter = 3 chi = 3.28 feet
1 nautical mile = 1.85 kilometers = 3.70 li = 1.15 miles

Units of Area

1 square kilometer = 100 hectares = 4 square li = 0.39 square miles
1 square meter = 9 square chi = 10.76 square feet
1 qing = 100 mu = 6.67 hectares
1 mu = 60 square zhang = 6.67 acres

Units of Weight

1 kilogram = 2 jin = 2.21 pounds

Units of Capacity

1 liter = 1 sheng = 0.22 gallons

Units of Weight and Measures[7]

Chinese System	Metric Equivalent	British Equivalent
LENGTH		
1 fen (10 li)		
1 cun (10 fen)	3.33 cm	1.31 inch
1 chi (10 cun)	0.33 m	1.09 foot
1 zhang (10 chi)	3.33 m	3.65 yard
1 li (150 zhang)	500 m	0.31 mile
AREA		
1 chi^2 (100 cun^2)	0.11 m^2	1.20 ft^2
1 zhang^2 (100 chi^2)	11.11 m^2	13.30 yd^2
1 li (22,500 zhang^2)	0.25 km^2	1.00 mi^2
1 fen (6 zhang^2)	66.67 m^2	79.73 yd^2
1 mu (10 fen)	6.67 ares	0.16 ac
1 qing (100 mu)	6.67 ha	16.47 ac
VOLUME		
1 chi^3 (1,000 cun^3)	0.04 m^3	1.31 ft^3
1 zhang^3 (1,000 chi^3)	37.04 m^3	1,308 ft^3
1 he	1 deciliter	0.18 pt
1 sheng (10 he)	1 l	0.22 gal
1 dou (10 sheng)	10 l	2.20 gal
WEIGHT		
1 shi (10 dou)	100 l	2.75 bu
1 qian	5 g	0.18 oz
1 liang (10 qian)	50 g	1.76 oz
1 jin (10 liang)	0.5 kg	1.10 lb
1 dan (100 jin)	.05 t	110.23 lb

CHINESE CALENDARS AND HOLIDAYS

The international standard for dates is based on the Gregorian calendar, a 1582 modification (named after Pope Gregory XIII) of the Julian calendar established by Julius Caesar in ancient Rome. In China, two calendars are used: the lunar and the Gregorian, also referred to as *yin* and *yang* calendars or as the "agricultural calendar," which relates to the phases of the moon, and the "national calendar" respectively. There is also a traditional Chinese lunisolar calendar, which tracks both lunar and seasonal changes.

Most traditional Chinese festivals are based on the lunar calendar. For example, the Chinese New Year falls on the first day of the first lunar month and typically is in late January or early February. When planning your trip, take note of these special occasions as flights may be very full and your business counterpart will not be available. Below are the key holidays in China that fall on the same date or period every year:[8]

January 1: New Year's Day (1 day off)
Late January or early February: Chinese New Year
    (3 days off)
May 1–3: International Labor Day (3 days off)
October 1–3: National Day (3 days off)

2

CULTURE SHOCK, JET LAG, AND FREE TIME

Culture Shock

If this is your first trip to China, you are probably looking forward to new and exotic experiences. Unfortunately, when you arrive, instead of feeling excited and energetic, you may end up feeling depressed, disoriented, and homesick, especially if you are traveling alone. This phenomenon is known as "culture shock." Here is what other women have to say about their experiences of culture shock in China:

- *On the traffic*: "When you drive down the street, the traffic is horrendous—bumper to bumper even at 10 P.M. Someone told me there are 1,000 new cars added to the streets each day. The whole time my driver is on the horn. Chinese drivers use the shoulder or cross lanes. It is sea of humanity moving through the streets—an amazing experience."

- *On the weather:* "Nobody told me anything about the extreme weather. Beijing is on the edge of the Gobi Desert, so it gets really hot—up to 95 degrees in April. When the dust storms come, you can hardly see what's 10 feet in front of you."
- *On hygiene:* "The worst culture shock for me was the lack of cleanliness. I saw a lot of spitting. The restrooms were not clean. I was in a city full of *hutongs* (a compound of houses around a courtyard), and there was one restroom for seven *hutongs*. You go to the market, and animals are strewn on the counter. . . . You are in a public area, and there are literally hundreds of people waiting in line for a restroom. You have no personal space. People move in masses."
- *On customer service:* "When you go to restaurant, a dumpling shop, or to a street vendor, the customers are often rude and the waitress is mean. There does not seem to be a concept of politeness. Customers bang their cups on the table and have loud arguments in public."
- *On beggars:* "One time, I was bitten by a homeless girl. There are many people who beg for money from foreigners. The little girl asked for money and reached into my pocket. When I grabbed her wrist, she bit me and ran away. I felt like it was organized begging from the rural villages. I noted that at the end of the day the group would head out from the rural areas and each morning send in women, children, and older men to beg."

For many Americans in foreign countries, the language barrier is often the most difficult issue to cope with. If you do not know even basic Chinese phrases, you will feel very isolated. How do you communicate with others to find a place to eat or to find your way around town? The street signs are in

Chinese, as are the names on shops and menus. What do you do for entertainment? The movies are in a foreign language and there are few places available where you can socialize easily. You suddenly feel very alienated.

Exhaustion is also common when traveling. Jet lag can be debilitating. The greater the change in time, the longer it takes to adjust. In China you will find night and day completely reversed from home, and you probably will have to start business negotiations the very day you land. Major cities in China are very congested and have a higher level of noise and air pollution than you may be used to.

For many Western women, the lack of hygiene is a major source of stress. An executive from Sydney, Australia, lamented, "Hygiene was a shock for me. Buildings were deteriorated. Everywhere I went there was dirt and filth. Even when cleaning was done, it was done with dirty mops and water."

For others, coming home after an extended stay in China raises doubts about the way of life in their own countries: "I lived in China for work for a few years. I had reverse culture shock when I came back to the U.S. When you return from a place where people make do with very limited resources, you begin to see how excessively Americans live. That realization about your own culture and society was hard to deal with."

FEELINGS YOU MAY HAVE

Although culture shock can be overwhelming, keep your sense of humor. Remember that your friends and family are only a phone call or e-mail away. While exposure to a new culture can be temporarily unsettling, being aware of what you are experiencing and knowing a few techniques to deal with it will help you enjoy your visit.

- *Depression:* When you have to deal with many people speaking a foreign tongue in a different culture, it is easy to become anxious and irritable. Feelings of helplessness can lead to depression and an overall loss of energy.

- *Disorientation:* Panic can set in quickly as you travel where English is not used on street signs, office buildings, or in restaurants. It is not only very frustrating to try to find your way in an unfamiliar environment, but also frightening when you don't recognize where you are and realize that you can't just ask anyone for help.
- *Intimidation:* We all like to feel that we are organized and in control of our environment. In China, you may feel frustrated and thwarted by the numerous steps it can take to perform a simple task such as paying for a purchase.
- *Alienation:* When you travel abroad, you may feel out of place, particularly if you don't speak the language. It is not likely that you will be invited to join a social group or be approached at a social gathering. You will more likely be left on your own, which may cause you to feel rejected and uncertain about how to proceed.
- *Boredom:* Because of language difficulties, there are not many places you can easily visit in the evenings or on weekends. If you don't speak the local language and are unsure about transportation, even taking a shopping trip might turn out to be a challenge.
- *Exhaustion:* You expend more energy doing less when you are on the road. Adjusting to jet lag, getting to your business appointments, maneuvering through crowds on the street, finding a cab, and haggling over prices can be physically and mentally exhausting.

TECHNIQUES FOR ADJUSTMENT

Recognize that any negative feelings you're experiencing in this new culture are normal. It's helpful to know that others have similar reactions. Remind yourself that you are traveling for a purpose and that you'll be going home when your job is done. Here are some suggestions to help you adjust to culture shock and jet lag:

- *Don't mope around your hotel room.* Stay active—jog, swim, or join a local exercise group if you have an extended stay. Take a walk through a local park or visit a museum. Re-center yourself by focusing on your strengths and pursuing your interests.
- *Relax.* When noise and crowds overwhelm you, take some time out for yourself. Consider bringing a relaxation tape with you to listen to for twenty minutes a day. Indulge in a bubble bath.
- *Create a personal touch.* If you are traveling for an extended period of time, try bringing a few things from home to put in your hotel room, such as photos, your favorite pillow, and maybe some of your favorite CDs to play while walking around. Newer model MP3 players such as the video iPod are ideal space savers, as you can carry a variety of music, photos, language lessons, and audio books in one device.
- *Travel with a companion.* If you know someone else who is also traveling on business, coordinate your schedules to meet for dinner or for sightseeing. It is easier to face a new environment as a team than to do it alone.
- *Ask your hosts questions about their country and culture.* They will usually enjoy talking about it, which will help you better understand and appreciate what you are seeing.
- *Be patient.* People in China are not usually as direct or in as much of a rush as people in the U.S. When you feel yourself getting uptight, take a few deep breaths and visualize a calming scene. Remember that people won't behave the way you expect or want them to, and getting upset won't make you or them feel any better.

- *Keep an open mind.* Look for similarities and intriguing differences between your culture and China's.
- *Try role reversal.* How would you react if a Chinese businessperson visiting you in the United States insisted that their way of living and doing business was the only way? When you're in another country, remember to do as the locals do, since it is your ways that may seem strange or offensive to them.
- *Know you are envied.* Many people would love having the opportunity to visit and conduct business in an exotic culture like China. They would give their eye teeth to be in your position. This should bring you some sense of satisfaction.
- *Keep your sense of humor.* Look for the amusing aspects of your situation. At least you will have lots of good stories to tell when you get home. When you feel confused, embarrassed, or upset, smile, smile, smile.

Jet Lag

Jet lag—a temporary disruption of bodily rhythms caused by high-speed travel across several time zones—is a physical challenge for many travelers. When we cross three or more time zones, either eastward or westward, we disrupt our body's sleeping, waking, and eating routines.

COPING WITH JET LAG

Jet lag affects people differently, and there are many remedies, rituals, and even medications, such as melatonin, available to help you ease jet lag. The key is to establish a routine that will work for you. It is important to quickly integrate into the new time zone starting from when you are on the plane. To do this, immediately set your watch to the local time, go to bed when it is dark in the new time zone, and force yourself to stay awake during daylight hours. Also consider the following tips:

- Try not to think about what time it is back home. Think in your new country's time zone.
- When you arrive, take a long walk or exercise in your hotel's facilities. This will help your circulation after a long flight, as well as tire you enough to promote a good night's sleep.
- A long, relaxing bath or a hot shower will help you sleep better.
- If you arrive in the daytime, stay up and wait until dark before going to bed. If you arrive at night, go to bed immediately so you can get up in the morning.
- Set an alarm clock to adjust to local time. A workout in the morning can help you acclimate to the new time zone.

FLYING COMFORTABLY

For travelers coming from the United States, the flight to China is very long. A direct flight from New York to Beijing is almost eighteen hours, and to a western city like Kunming (Yunnan Province) it is twenty-seven hours long with three stops in between. If you will have time to check in to your hotel before your first meeting, then a light sweatshirt and walking shoes are most comfortable for the flight. They will also come in handy if you have time later in the trip for an evening walk around the city. If you must head directly to a meeting after landing, consider wearing comfortable attire on board, then changing clothes in the airplane bathroom or in the airport when you arrive. If you belong to an airline club, check if they have shower facilities you can use upon arrival, as you may need to make reservations in advance. Here are more tips for flying comfortably:

- Eat lightly the night before you fly and on the plane to adjust to a different meal schedule.
- Drink a lot of water, as flying is very dehydrating. Water will help reduce fatigue and headaches that can come with long flights.
- Avoid alcohol on the plane, which is dehydrating and can throw off your sleep cycle.
- Wear loose clothing and try to stretch or walk around a few times while on board to improve your circulation and avoid leg cramps.
- Take off your shoes and wear a pair of socks while flying. Your feet will probably swell, and tight shoes will become uncomfortable.
- Your ears may clog during descent and landing, which is a common problem on long flights. Chewing gum and yawning may provide relief. Quickly drinking carbonated water may help as well. Another approach is the Valsalva maneuver: Hold your nose and keep your mouth open, while gently blowing out with a few short breaths. This causes the ears to pop. Taking a decongestant pill or using a saline nasal spray two hours before you take off and fifteen minutes before you land will help you clear your breathing passage.
- If you wear contact lenses, bring a spare pair, or if you wear disposable lenses, bring extras in addition to your glasses. You may find that contacts become dry in your eyes while you are on board the plane. It is best to take them out for the flight and wear glasses. If you do wear lenses during the flight, keep lubricating drops handy and use them frequently.
- Bring a neck pillow and sleep mask (most travel stores

carry them) to help you sleep, especially if you have a center seat on the plane. Keep eyedrops, toothbrush and toothpaste, lip balm, eye cream (there are also rehydrating eye patches), and a face toner in your purse to help you feel refreshed during the flight.

Free Time

It is inevitable when you travel that things won't all go according to plan. You will probably experience delays and may end up having lots of free time. You might have a long waiting time in between flights. You might also find that a meeting has been canceled or rescheduled when you arrive. Or, you might have your evenings entirely free while in China. In general, be prepared for unexpected free time.

- Keep a book, magazines, and computer devices nearby to help pass the time. It can be very frustrating to sit in an airport with an extended delay and only one English newspaper available for sale at the newsstand. Internet access is fairly available in most major hotels in Shanghai and Beijing and most have wireless lobbies and executive floors. Connection rates may be more expensive than at other destinations. If you use a corporate VPN (Virtual Private Network) then your data and e-mails will be secure. Public access to the Internet is not secure. so assume that anything you type—passwords, personal records, etc.—can be viewed by others. The Chinese government has installed the "Great Firewall of China" that blocks various Web sites and blogs.
- Bring a CD or MP3 player with your favorite music or, even better, language lessons for the country you are visit-

ing. It will help pass the time and help you learn some key phrases. If you are using batteries, don't forget to pack extras.

- Depending on the duration of your stay in China and how heavy your phone usage will be, there are several options for cell phone use. If you already have a GSM phone, check with your provider to see whether your cell service will work in China and if so, in what cities and how much the costs will be to place calls and roam. Roaming charges can quickly become prohibitive, so another option is to use a local SIM card that you can get in the airport upon arrival. This will convert your phone to a local phone number so you are charged only local fees. Another option is to buy a phone and prepaid cell phone service upon your arrival in China. Details of these options are easily available on the Web for further research.

- Many airports have services for business travelers who are delayed. Some excellent stop-over points include Heathrow Airport in London, England; Frankfurt International Airport, Germany; and the Changi Airport, Singapore. Services may include health clubs, showers, swimming pools, movies, city tours, and nap rooms.

- If you plan to travel a lot, it is wise to join one of the many airline hospitality clubs. These clubs provide a quiet area to relax during a long delay. Many of these hospitality clubs offer refreshments and other amenities such as TV and magazines. Check whether you are eligible for a one-time use of a club at an international airport. If you are flying business or first class, club entry is usually complimentary.

- Check to see if any museums or department stores in the city have late-night hours. This can be a great time to catch up on shopping and to get a massage or spa treatment at affordable prices.

EXPLORING ON YOUR OWN

When you are in China, you may have a chance to explore on your own. Make full use of the opportunity. Here are some tips for helping you get around:

- Take a city tour shortly after you arrive, which is a great way to learn about the culture and meet other business-women on the road. Many hotels offer nightlife tours that include a city tour, dinner, and cultural show. Many of these excursions can be booked the same day so you can fit them into your busy schedule on short notice.
- Do a little bit of sightseeing each day you are in China. Visiting even one city site on the way back to your hotel from a meeting or on the way to lunch or dinner will help you gain a deeper understanding of the culture and people.
- If the area is safe for walking (ask at the hotel), get a map and explore. Your hotel will provide a map of the surrounding area at your request. A walk through the neighborhood will help you see how people live and work. Be smart about walking and do so only during daylight hours and in safe areas.
- Hire a driver or use a taxi. In China prices are reasonable. Renting a car would be more than you can or would want to handle. The public train system in big cities like Shanghai is also convenient and safe.
- Plan your travel routes. Keep the telephone numbers of taxi services, bus and train route maps, as well as a card from your hotel in the local language in case you get lost. City maps can easily be obtained from tourist offices at the airport or from your hotel concierge.
- Establish familiar grounds if you are there for an extended period of travel. Frequent certain lunch and dinner spots and evening hangouts to help you establish a rapport with

the owners and locals. It will help make you feel like you're part of the group.

- Talk to locals who speak English. They appreciate the chance to practice their English and will be delighted by your interest in their culture. Locals will be more than happy to answer your questions about China.

DINING ALONE

The reality for many businesswomen is that they are on the road for long periods of time alone. Hence, eating alone while traveling is inevitable. Dining in China can be an intimidating experience if you do not speak Mandarin, so many women resort to ordering room service every night. As one businesswoman lamented, it is harder to order food in China than in Japan because Japanese restaurants at least offer pictures to point to if you don't speak the language.

In major cities like Beijing and Shanghai, dining out should not be a concern, as hotels will provide a list of good restaurants. Many of these are top-notch and will certainly provide an English menu and excellent service. You will also find Western chains such as Starbucks, McDonald's, Subway, and Pizza Hut. Nearby shopping centers offer an array of food choices that you will be glad to sample. You can even takeout food and dine in the comfort of your hotel room.

In less developed cities in China, however, dining can be more of a challenge. A safe bet is to dine at restaurants within the hotel chain at which you are staying, but be prepared that you may not find such convenient choices in the more remote cities. If that is the case, approach the hotel concierge for suggestions on the nearest eating places and have the directions written down. Remember to ask the hotel for an address card so that you can return without a problem. Here are some additional tips:

- Dine in other business hotels in the area, which usually have many types of restaurants and are accustomed to individual diners.
- Many upscale hotels have lounge areas, some with a piano player, that offer seating for one and a menu of light snacks at all hours.
- Several hotels offer night dining tours so you can take a city tour and dine with other people while enjoying the local culture.
- Some of the better hotels have concierge floors that provide good views, wireless technology, ample reading materials, and TV, and many offer a light dinner and breakfast that is popular with busy business travelers.
- Some cities have dinner theater shows so you can dine while watching the theater and meet other travelers.

SHOPPING

If you have free time, grab the opportunity to shop around the city. You will likely find great bargains that you won't get back home in the U.S. You can choose to shop at department stores and mega-malls that have sprung up all over China, or, if you are the adventurous type, venture into local stalls and boutiques. It is best to go with a companion, as it is safer and you can have fun bargaining together. Better still, your host might offer to take you on an evening shopping spree.

Here are some of the top items that travelers in China shop for:

- Custom-made clothing (suits, jackets, dresses)
- Silk (children's outfits, scarves, clothing, ties, accessories, comforters)
- Jewelry (jade, gold, silver, pearls)
- Cloisonné (enamel jewelry)
- Antiques and artifacts (coins, statues, replicas)

- Writing and painting items (brushes, paper, framed calligraphy)
- Chinese tea and tea sets
- Local arts and crafts
- Imitation designer goods (watches, purses, clothes, etc.)

TOP TOURIST SITES

Here is a list of top tourist sites that you should try to visit in Beijing, Shanghai, and Hong Kong.

Beijing

- The Great Wall
- Tiananmen Gate/Square
- The Forbidden City
- The Summer Palace
- The Temple of Heaven
- Bei Hai Park
- The Ming Tombs
- The Peking Man
- Lama Temple
- Panda House at Beijing Zoo
- Radio TV Tower
- Hutongs
- Fahai Temple
- Former Residence of Soong Ching Ling
- Ban Bi Dan Forest Park
- Bell Tower and Drum Tower
- Peking Opera

Shanghai

- The Bund
- Nanjing Road
- Yuyuan Gardens

- Gu Yi Garden
- Oriental Pearl TV Tower
- Jade Buddha Monastery
- Huai Hai Road
- People's Square
- Shanghai Art Museum
- Great World Entertainment Center
- Huang Pu River Tour
- Shanghai Museum

Hong Kong

- Victoria Peak and the Peak Tram Ride
- Stanley Market
- Star Ferry boat ride in Victoria Harbour
- Repulse Bay
- Ocean Park
- Jumbo floating restaurants in Aberdeen
- Wong Tai Sin Temple
- Giant Buddha
- Temple Street
- Statue Square
- Hong Kong and Shanghai Bank Building

HEALTH ISSUES WHEN TRAVELING

By Pamela Galley, RN, Chapman University

In the past twenty years, China has made considerable progress in improving health standards, even in the rural areas. Overall, people in China are living longer and healthier lives, and contemporary business travelers face fewer health concerns when traveling to China than they did twenty years ago. However, for women especially, it remains important to be aware of the necessary precautions to take when traveling to a still developing country like China.

Medical Preparation

PRE-TRAVEL PHYSICAL EXAMINATION

If you are planning to visit China, see your doctor at least four to six weeks before your trip to allow for shots to take effect.

If you have less than four weeks before you leave, it may not be too late to get your shots or medication, so you should still see your doctor. Seek advice on how to protect yourself from illnesses and injuries while traveling abroad. Ask your doctor about your risk factor for developing deep vein thrombosis (see "Health Risks," below).

CARRYING MEDICATION

If you travel with preexisting medical problems, carry a letter from your doctor describing your condition, including information about any prescription medicines that you must take. You should also have the generic names of the drugs, preferably translated into Chinese before you go.

Leave medications in their original labeled containers in your carry-on luggage to make customs processing easier. If you have allergies, reactions to certain medication, or other unique medical problems, you may consider wearing a medical alert bracelet or carrying a similar warning.[9] Be sure to bring along over-the-counter diarrhea medication (e.g., bismuth subsalicylate, loperamide) and an antibiotic prescribed by your doctor to self-treat moderate to severe diarrhea. Make sure you have enough prescription medication to last during your trip.

If you have been ill while traveling, notify your doctor upon return. If you become ill within one year of returning home with any of the following symptoms, see your doctor: a fever or flu-like illness, persistent or intermittent diarrhea, a skin rash or sores, jaundice (typically noticed when the whites of the eyes appear yellow), unexplained weight loss, shortness of breath, or fatigue.

PREGNANCY

If you are pregnant, talk to your doctor before making travel arrangements. Notify the airline of your pregnancy. A medical certificate may be required if you will be traveling within four weeks of your delivery date in a normal, uncomplicated pregnancy. According to guidelines issued by American Airlines, international travel is not advised within thirty days of the due date, unless you are examined by an obstetrician within forty-eight hours of outbound departure and are certified in writing as medically stable for flight.[10] Check with the specific airline you are taking for restrictions on travel.

A child born abroad to a U.S. citizen generally acquires U.S. citizenship at birth. As soon as possible after the birth, the American parent or parents should contact the nearest U.S. embassy or consulate to have a "Report of Birth Abroad of a Citizen of the United States of America" prepared. This document serves as proof of U.S. citizenship and is acceptable evidence for obtaining a U.S. passport.[11]

Health Risks

AVIAN INFLUENZA ("BIRD FLU")

Since almost all human cases of avian influenza have occurred in those who have had direct contact with live infected poultry or sustained and intimate contact with family members suffering from the disease, the risk to travelers is extremely low. Avoid exposure to live poultry, including visits to poultry farms and open markets with live birds.

DEEP VEIN THROMBOSIS

DVT is a serious condition involving blood clots in the legs. Sometimes these clots can break away and travel the bloodstream to vital organs of the body. In the lungs, a clot can cause pulmonary embolism (PE). Prolonged physical immobility, such as sitting still for an extended period, is associated with DVT. The World Health Organization (WHO) considers the link between air travel and DVT probable but small, and believes it mainly affects passengers who are already at risk. WHO recommends leg exercises during travel. Taking occasional walks during a long flight increases blood circulation in the legs.

The following past and current medical conditions may induce DVT: blood clotting disorders, cancer, oral contraceptive use or hormone therapy, heart disease or other vascular disease, obesity, pregnancy, recent major surgery or trauma (e.g., within the past six weeks), and varicose veins. Talk to your doctor if you believe you are at risk for DVT.

TRAVELERS' DIARRHEA

Make sure your food and drinking water are safe. Food and waterborne diseases are the primary cause of illness among international travelers. Infections may cause diarrhea and vomiting (E. coli, Salmonella, cholera, and parasites), fever (typhoid fever and toxoplasmosis), or liver damage (hepatitis). Avoid buying food or drink from street vendors. Most doctors recommend taking only clear liquids for the first 24–48 hours. The nonprescription remedy bismuth subsalicylate (Pepto-Bismol, Bismatrol, or Bismed) has been shown to decrease the duration and severity of diarrhea by about 60 percent. For diarrhea, take one fluid ounce or two tablets every thirty minutes for up to eight doses in a 24-hour period, which can be repeated daily. People who use aspirin products should not use it. Watch for signs of dehydration, such as dry mouth and dark-colored urine. See a doctor if symptoms do not resolve within forty-eight hours or if you have a high fever or signs of dehydration. Most cases resolve within one to three days without medical treatment.

SEVERE ACUTE RESPIRATORY SYNDROME (SARS)

SARS usually begins with a high fever of more than 100.4 degrees Fahrenheit (38 degrees Celsius). It is followed by headache, body aches, and mild respiratory difficulties. Some patients may suffer diarrhea. One week after the onset of these symptoms, SARS patients develop a dry cough which may worsen into pneumonia. As SARS is spread through close person-to-person contact (e.g., touching a door knob that a SARS patient had touched), it is important to clean your hands regularly with soap and water. Bring disinfecting wipes with you for convenience.

In the spring of 2003, an unprecedented global public health response was launched to eliminate SARS. Although SARS was beaten back less than eight months after it first started taking lives, this epidemic exposed weaknesses in China's disease control and surveillance system, health facility control, and medical scientific research. It raised questions about the structure of China's public health system, and demonstrated how two decades of underfunded health care have left the country unprepared for public health emergencies.

Immunizations

Before travel, be sure you are up to date on all routine immunizations according to schedules approved by the Advisory Committee on Immunization Practice (ACIP). Some schedules can be accelerated for travel. Check your health care records to ensure measles, mumps, rubella, polio, diphtheria, tetanus, and pertussis immunizations are up to date. No immunizations are needed to return to the U.S. Although vaccinations are not required, vaccines against the following may be recommended:

- *Hepatitis A or immune globulin (IG):* Transmission of hepatitis A virus can occur through direct person-to-person contact, exposure to contaminated water, ice, or shellfish harvested in contaminated water, or from fruits, vegetables, or other foods that are eaten uncooked and contaminated during harvesting or subsequent handling.
- *Hepatitis:* Recommended if you might be exposed to blood or body fluids (for example, health-care workers), have sexual contact with the local population, or be exposed through medical treatment.
- *Japanese encephalitis:* Recommended if you plan to visit rural farming areas and under special circumstances, such as a known outbreak of Japanese encephalitis.
- *Rabies:* Recommended if you will have extensive unprotected outdoor exposure in rural areas, which might occur during camping, hiking, or cycling, or engagement in certain occupational activities.
- *Typhoid:* Typhoid fever can be contracted through contaminated drinking water or food. Large outbreaks are most often related to fecal contamination of water supplies or foods sold by street vendors.

Discuss your travel plans and personal health with a health care provider to determine which vaccines you will need. For general travel health information, check the Web site of the Centers for Disease Control and Prevention (CDC) at www.cdc.gov/travel or the Web site of the World Health Organization (WHO) Web site at www.who.int/en/.

Health Facilities

By the end of 2003, there were 305,000 health care institutions in China, including 64,000 hospitals and health care stations, 3,058 maternal and child health care institutions, and 1,811 specialized health institutions or stations. Hospitals and health care institutions had a total capacity of 2.9 million beds, and there were 4.24 million health workers, including 1.83 million practicing and assistant doctors and 1.24 million registered nurses. Reforms are underway to expand the coverage of the urban insurance system and to improve the efficiency of service delivery, but excessive usage fees still characterize the existing health service system in China.

Western-style medical facilities with international staffs are available in Beijing, Shanghai, Guangzhou, and a few other large cities. Many hospitals in major Chinese cities have so-called VIP wards (*gaogan bingfang*). These feature reasonably up-to-date medical technology and the most skilled physicians. Most VIP wards also provide medical services to foreigners and have English-speaking doctors and nurses. Most hospitals in China will not accept medical insurance from the United States, with the exception of the following hospitals, which are on BlueCross BlueShield's worldwide network providers of overseas hospitals.

- Hong Kong Adventist Hospital
- Beijing United Family Hospital
- International Medical Center in Beijing
- Peking Union Medical Center

Travelers will be asked to place a deposit prior to admission to cover the expected cost of treatment. Hospitals in major cities may accept credit cards for payment. Even in the VIP/

foreigner wards of major hospitals, however, American patients have frequently encountered difficulty obtaining proper medical care due to cultural and regulatory differences. Physicians and hospitals sometimes refuse to supply American patients with complete copies of their Chinese hospital medical records, including laboratory test results, scans, and X-rays. All Americans traveling to China are strongly encouraged to buy foreign medical care and medical evacuation insurance prior to arrival.[12]

HEALTH INSURANCE

Obtaining medical treatment and hospital care can be costly for travelers who are injured or who become seriously ill overseas. U.S. medical insurance plans seldom cover health costs incurred outside the United States unless supplemental coverage is purchased. U.S. Social Security Medicare and Medicaid programs do *not* provide payment for hospital or medical services outside the United States.

Before you leave the United States, you should be informed about which medical services your health insurance will cover abroad. If your health insurance policy does not provide coverage for hospital or medical costs abroad, you are urged to purchase a temporary health policy that provides this type of coverage. There are short-term health and emergency assistance policies designed for travelers.

Many travel agents and private companies offer insurance plans that will cover health care expenses incurred overseas, including emergency services such as medical evacuations. Uninsured travelers who require medical care overseas often face extreme difficulties. When consulting with your insurer prior to your trip, ascertain whether payment will be made to the overseas health care provider or if you will be reimbursed later for expenses you incur.

Beijing SOS International in Beijing City offers medical insurance policies designed for travelers and has staff in China who can assist in the event of a medical emergency.

Beijing SOS International, Ltd.
1 North Road, Xingfu Sancun Sanlitun, Chaoyang District, Beijing 100027
24-Hour Emergency anywhere in China: (8610) 6462-9100
24-Hour Emergency from Hong Kong: (852) 2528-9900
24-Hour Emergency from the U.S.: (215) 245-4707
Telephone in China: (8610) 6462-9112
Facsimile in China: (8610) 6462-9111
Insurance information in the U.S. (M–F 8:30–4:30 EST): (800) 523-8930
E-mail: china.marketing@internationalsos.com

EMERGENCIES
For all emergencies, dial 120 from anywhere in China for emergency medical service, and 110 for all other emergencies. If you become ill or injured while abroad, contact the nearest U.S. embassy or consulate for a list of local doctors, dentists, medical specialists, clinics, and hospitals. If your illness or injury is serious, the U.S. consul can help you find medical assistance and at your request inform your family or friends of your condition. If necessary, a consul can assist in the transfer of funds from the United States. Payment of hospital or other expenses is your responsibility. U.S. consular officers cannot supply you with medication.[13]

Ambulances do not carry sophisticated medical equipment, and ambulance personnel generally have little or no medical training. Therefore, injured or seriously ill Americans may be required to take taxis or other immediately available vehicles to the nearest major hospital rather than wait for ambulances to arrive. Although some health insurance companies may pay "customary and reasonable" hospital costs abroad, very few will pay for medical evacuation back to the United States.

Beijing United Family Hospital and Clinics
2 Jiang Tai Lu, Chao Yang District, Beijing 100016
Telephone: (010) 6433-3960/1/2/4/5
Facsimile: (010) 6433-3963
Emergency hotline: (010)6433-2345

Peking Union Medical Hospital
1 Shui Fu yuan, Dong Cheng District, Beijing 100730
24-Hour Emergency: (010) 6529-6114
Telephone: (010) 6529-7292

WHO Representative in the People's Republic of China
World Health Organization China Office, 401 Dongwai Diplomatic Office Building, No. 23 Dongzhimenwai Avenue, Chaoyang District, Beijing 100600
Telephone: 0086-01-65327189 to 92
Facsimile: 0086-01-65322359

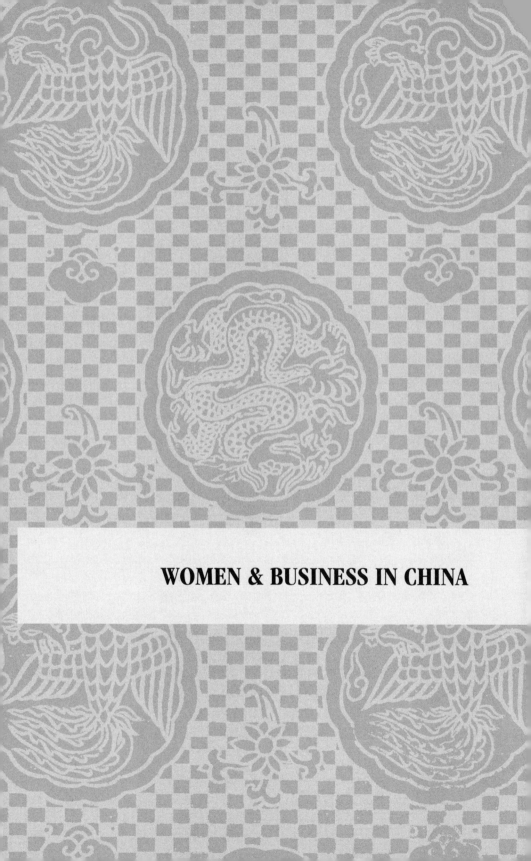

WOMEN & BUSINESS IN CHINA

BUSINESS AND GOVERNMENT IN CHINA

By Yuen Yuen Ang, Stanford University

Doing business in China almost always involves doing business with the government. People in the government, rather than the law, exercise significant authority on such matters as who can invest, where, and in what manner. Oftentimes local officials and state-appointed managers are the very people with whom you need to make a deal. Therefore, understanding the political and regulatory landscape in China is essential to your business success. For Western businesswomen especially, learning to navigate the bureaucracy can greatly enhance your standing as a foreign investor and negotiator. This chapter arms you with basic knowledge of business and government in China. You will learn about the structure of authority in the Chinese government, followed by an overview of key issues in foreign investment. A list of "what's what" and "who's who" offers a quick reference to must-know organizations and people in China.

Structure of the Chinese Government

China is a one-party state led by the Chinese Communist Party (CCP). In theory, China is a centralized and hierarchical political system, but in reality it is highly decentralized. Kenneth Lieberthal and David Lampton describe China's system as "fragmented authoritarianism," where "authority below the very peak of the Chinese political system is fragmented and disjointed."[14] The result of this fragmentation is an endless "bargaining treadmill" among different governmental authorities and businesses.[15] Foreigners who conduct business in China should be prepared for a process of negotiation that is "disjointed, protracted, and incremental."[16]

DIVISION OF AUTHORITY IN CHINA

Understanding the division of power is essential to identifying who has the say over your business endeavors. Broadly speaking, there are three lines of division in the Chinese political system.

- First, political authority is divided between party and government. At each level of administration, there is a party secretary and governmental head (e.g., governor, mayor, township leader, etc.) in charge. Sometimes they are the same person. It is common to meet an official who hands you a name card with multiple titles. Sometimes the party and governmental official are two different people holding more or less equal decision-making power.
- Second, China is something of a de facto federal system divided into five administrative layers: central, province, prefecture, county, and township. The horizontal separation of powers is what the Chinese call *kuai*. In theory, the lower-level administration (e.g., province) is subordinate

to the higher-level administration (e.g., central). In reality, however, each level of administration may exercise autonomy from higher levels depending on the particular policy area. Provincial governments, for example, have acquired considerable control over investment and business-related issues.

- Third, the Chinese state is also divided vertically into different ministries, departments, and bureaus, based on functions, known as *tiao*. There are twenty-eight ministries and commissions in the current administration, each with a subordinated group of departments and bureaus. This vertical structure is then replicated at each level of administration, forming a matrix, as illustrated here:

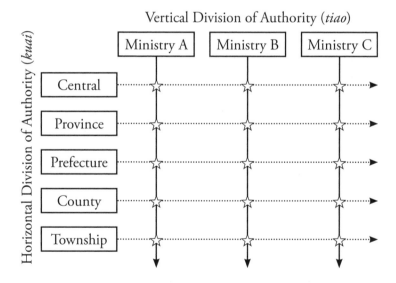

State-owned and collective-owned enterprises (SOEs), public service units (PSUs), and banks all come under the authority of the state. Many governmental organizations create spin-off companies or public service units (PSUs). There were over one million PSUs in China in 2002, employing thirty million professional staff and ranging across all sectors of the economy.[17] Since many of these PSUs operate almost like private companies, you may unknowingly be doing business with a government-linked organization.

IMPACT ON BUSINESS NEGOTIATIONS

The division of authority in the government affects your business negotiations. As a reflection of the matrix system, each Chinese official (as indicated by the star in in the chart on page 65) is answerable to the horizontal authority (e.g., provincial government) and vertical authority (e.g., Ministry of Finance) at the same time. Sometimes the two authorities can disagree, in which case obtaining approval for your business and getting past the bureaucracy can pose difficulties.

The level of administration at which you do business will also affect who your negotiating partners are. For example, if you are planning to acquire a public enterprise at a particular township, you may have to negotiate with the township party secretary, township official, and factory manager. Depending on the size of your project, higher level officials may get involved. In short, when dealing with the Chinese government, be prepared for a sizable entourage and protracted process of negotiation. For more tips on negotiating with the Chinese, please refer to Chapter 6.

Foreign Investment in China

China is no doubt one of the top destinations for foreign direct investment (FDI) in the world today. In 2005 the actual value of FDI reached US$72.4 billion, posting an impressive

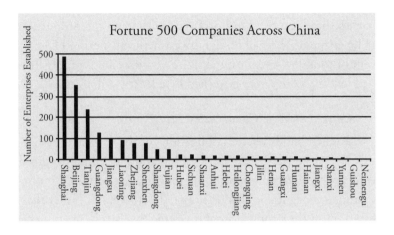

Fortune 500 Companies Across China

increase of nearly 20 percent from 2004. Within the first four months of 2006, 12,639 foreign-funded investment projects were approved. Foreign companies account for 88 percent of China's high-tech exports.[18] Among the Fortune 500 companies in 2002, more than 400 have already invested in China.

The chart above shows the distribution of enterprises established by Fortune 500 companies throughout China from 1979 to 2002.[19] Shanghai, Beijing, and Tianjin are the top three spots for FDI, with Shanghai alone attracting 491 such enterprises. Among these foreign companies, 73 percent are in the manufacturing industry and only 27 percent are in the services and commercial sectors.

MODES OF FOREIGN DIRECT INVESTMENT
There are five major modes of foreign investment in China. Each is based on a distinct set of contractual terms and establishment requirements.

Equity Joint Venture (hezi)
In an equity joint venture, a foreign company invests and manages the enterprise jointly with a Chinese company. Both

parties share the risks and profits according to the proportion of investment. Share of foreign investment must exceed 25 percent of total registered capital. Joint ventures are typically limited liability companies governed by a Board of Directors.

Contractual or Cooperative Joint Venture (hezuo)

Rights, liabilities, and obligations of the foreign and Chinese investing parties are decided based on a mutually agreed contract. Unlike an equity joint venture, the terms of profit-sharing are negotiated and contracted beforehand, rather than based upon the proportion of investment. Usually in cooperative joint ventures, the foreign company provides the capital, while the Chinese counterpart provides the physical assets and labor.

Wholly Owned Foreign Enterprise (duzi)

This type of enterprise is invested in and owned solely by a foreign company, who has exclusive rights to the management and profits of the enterprise.

Joint-stock Limited Liability Enterprise (gufen)

All of the capital of the enterprise is composed of equal value shares. Shares purchased by foreign companies must exceed 25 percent of the total registered capital.

Transfer of Management Rights

In this form of venture, foreign companies establish an enterprise by purchasing the shares and right of ownership of a Chinese enterprise (many of these are state-owned companies). Payment must be made to the Chinese company within three months of issuance of the license to the newly established foreign-funded enterprise. Management rights will only take effect after full payment has been made.

IMPORTANT ISSUES FOR FOREIGN INVESTORS

- Registration and approval requirements for foreign investment vary depending on the region in which you invest. Therefore, be sure to check with the appropriate regional department before you enter into negotiations.
- Depending on the total registered capital of your company and the type of project in which you engage, you will need to obtain approval from different agencies and different levels of government. For example, a project that is over US$30 million has to be approved by the Ministry of Foreign Trade and Economic Cooperation in Beijing rather than by the local economic bureau.
- Taxes are a major issue. Examine the local tax structure before you make business plans. There are usually tax incentives for foreigners in particular economic zones and provinces. For example, the Tianjin government offers favorable tax rates for foreign-funded high-tech enterprises. In Nankai District, foreign enterprises enjoy a two-year exemption on income taxes beginning with their first profitable year, and an additional fifty-percent exemption from the third to fifth year.
- The Chinese government plans to standardize enterprise income taxes between foreign and local companies as early as 2008. Foreign enterprises are currently taxed at a de facto rate of 13 to 17 percent, compared to 23 to 33 percent among locals. Official sources report that the unified tax rate is likely to be in the range of 24 to 27 percent, with a transition period of approximately five years.
- New regulations for mergers and acquisitions were implemented in September 2006. There are now tighter controls on attempts to acquire Chinese state-owned enterprises or established brand names.
- Watch out! The Chinese government has stepped up ef-

forts to audit foreign companies. A study conducted by Chinese Prosperity Supervision Center in 2002 found that one-third of the 3,200 representative offices in China have underreported their tax liabilities.

- Foreigners who work in China must apply for the Z-type visa. You must present a permit of employment issued by the local bureau of labor.

- Foreign enterprises must conform to the Chinese Labor Law. There are certain restrictions on dismissing and laying off Chinese employees. Foreign enterprises are also required to contribute to the social security fund (medical expenses, welfare benefits, and pension) of local employees.

- Talent recruitment and retention has become the top concern for foreign enterprises in China, as reported by the U.S.–China Business Council 2006 Annual Member Survey. A 2006 study conducted by Mercer Consulting of 114 companies in Greater China finds that more than half of the respondents have experienced increased turnover among professional staff. Replacement costs average 20 to 25 percent of annual salary per employee and up to 200 percent for senior executives.

- Foreign companies can now remit currency back home without going through the tedious approval process at the State Administration of Foreign Exchange (SAFE) for certain non-trade items, e.g., remuneration for expatriates, overseas business trip allowances, etc.

- To protect your intellectual property, you must register all your trademarks and patents on a "first-to-file" basis at the intellectual property office. By 2004 foreign companies had registered 230,000 patents in China, accounting for 87 percent in bioengineering and 90 percent in the pharmaceuticals field.

Who's Who and What's What

As part of your business preparation, it is helpful to be familiar with key personalities and organizations in the Chinese government and business sector. This basic knowledge can also help you make intelligent conversation and avoid embarrassing faux pas during social functions.

KEY PERSONALITIES: GOVERNMENT

- *Mao Zedong:* Mao was the paramount leader of Communist China, which he ruled from its establishment in 1945 to his death in 1976. Today, he remains revered in the official press as the founding father of the People's Republic of China.
- *Deng Xiaoping:* Deng was the second-generation patriarch following Mao. He instituted economic reforms beginning in the late 1970s. Deng is credited for directing China's phenomenal economic success.
- *Jiang Zemin:* Jiang was the third president of China. Jiang is known for his platform of "three represents" (*sangedaibiao*), which includes the embrace of private entrepreneurship in China's politics and economy.
- *Hu Jintao:* Hu is the top leader in China's current and fourth administration. He is president of the People's Republic of China, general secretary of the Communist Party, and chairman of the Central Military Commission. Hu places emphasis on promoting equitable growth in China.
- *Wen Jiabao:* Wen is the premier of the State Council. He leads the executive branch of government.
- *Wu Yi:* Wu is the only female member of the Politburo and a state councilor. She was appointed Minister of Health following the SARS epidemic.

- *Wang Qishan:* Mayor of Beijing City. You will likely catch him on TV during the 2008 Olympics. He is chairman of the organizing committee for the Beijing Olympic Games.
- *Han Zheng:* Mayor of Shanghai City. Shanghai is one of China's richest cities and the top destination for foreign direct investment.
- *Liu Mingkang:* Chairman of the board of directors of the People's Bank of China since 2000 and chairman of the China Banking Regulatory Commission. A native of Fujian province, he is an economist who graduated with an MBA from the University of London.
- *Zhou Xiaochuan:* Governor of the People's Bank of China since 2002. In 2000 he was also appointed chairman of the China Securities Regulatory Commission.
- *Wang Zhongfu:* Minister of the State Administration for Industry and Commerce (SIAC). SIAC is the leading agency for market regulation and is responsible for the registration of businesses, including foreign-invested enterprises.
- *Xie Xuren:* Director of the State Bureau of Taxation. As the name suggests, this is the bureaucracy in charge of tax issues.

KEY PERSONALITIES: BUSINESS

- *Wang Jiming:* President of the China National Petroleum Corporation, a state-owned company and the largest oil and gas company in China. As part of a national effort to expand energy resources, CNPC acquired PetroKazakhstan in 2005.
- *Zhang Reimin:* CEO of Haier Corporation, an electrical appliances manufacturer, which set up a factory in North Carolina.
- *Robin Li Yanhong:* Cofounder and CEO of Baidu.com,

the Chinese equivalent of Google. A graduate of the State University of New York, Li had previously worked at Dow Jones and Infoseek.

- *Rong Yiren & Family:* Founder of CITIC Group, one of the largest investment companies in China.
- *Liu Yongxing & Brothers:* Founders of the Hope Group, one of the largest private Chinese companies that produce animal feed.
- *Ren Zhengfei:* Founder of Huawei Technologies, which manufactures GSM cell phones and telecommunication equipment, worth $1.5 billion in annual revenue. Huawei has set up research facilities in America, Germany, and Sweden.
- *Wu Yijian:* Founder of Shaanxi Jinhua Qiye, one of China's most successful pharmaceutical companies.
- *Song Chaodi:* Founder of Kelihua (Clever) Software Group, a top player in China's lucrative education software market.

KEY ORGANIZATIONS

- *State Council* (guowuyuan): The State Council is the leading body of the executive branch of government, responsible for enacting policies and laws. It is led by the premier, followed by the vice premier, and then various ministers and commissioners.
- *Ministries and Commissions* (bu/weiyuanhui): These are the vertical authorities under the direction of the State Council, including the Ministry of Finance, Ministry of Labor and Social Security, Ministry of Foreign Trade and Economic Cooperation, and the People's Bank of China. Each is in charge of a regulatory function.
- *Politburo* (zhengzhi ju): The Politburo is composed of leading members of the Chinese Communist Party. It is

led by the general secretary—currently Hu Jintao—the top political position in China. Within the Politburo, the Standing Committee is a small group of the most powerful leaders in China. There are currently nine members in the Standing Committee, including President Hu Jintao and Premier Wen Jiabao.

* *Provincial Governments*: There are twenty-two provinces (including Guangdong, Fujian, and Hainan), four metropolises (Beijing, Shanghai, Chongqing, and Tianjin), and five autonomous regions (Tibet, Xinjiang, Inner Mongolia, Guangxi, and Ningxia) in China. Provincial governments are led by governors, who share the same political rank as ministers and commissioners.

In addition to the key institutions, the following is the general contact information for regulatory departments in Beijing that foreign businesses may visit.

DEPARTMENT   FUNCTION

National Development and Reform Commission
No. 38 Yuetan South Street, Xicheng District, Beijing
Web site (English): en.ndrc.gov.cn.

Economic Policy Coordination Department	Supervises financial and monetary policies; sets investment structure; manages price level; regulates issuance of bonds and enterprise funding.
Investment Department	Supervises macro investment policies; controls operation of fixed asset management and construction projects.

| Department of Foreign Capital Utilization | Supervises direct foreign investment; regulates major projects funded by foreign sources; monitors investment projects overseas. |
| Economic and Trade Circulation Department | Develops strategies for internal and external trade; formulates plans for export and imports; monitors commodities market. |

State Administration of Taxation
No. 5. Yangfangdian Xi Road, Haidian District, Beijing
Web site (Chinese): www.chinatax.gov.cn
Telephone: +86 010-63417114

| Department of Circulation Tax Administration | Collects and administers VAT (value-added tax), consumption tax, and business tax. |

State Administration for Industry and Commerce
No. 8 Sanheli East Road, Xicheng District, Beijing
Web site (English): gsyj.saic.gov.cn/wcm/WCMData/pub/saic/english/default.htm
Telephone: +86-10-68010463/68013447

| Foreign Funded Enterprise Registration Administration | Formulates measures on foreign investment enterprise registration; administers registration of foreign invested enterprises. |

State Intellectual Property Office
No. 6, Xitucheng Road, Jimen Bridge, Haidian District, Beijing
Web site (English): www.sipo.gov.cn/sipo_English/

| Administration of Patent | Reviews applications for patents; offers patent information service. |

For more information on key personalities and organizations in China, you may wish to visit the following Web sites: www.chinavitae.com (for background on hundreds of leading figures in the public and private sector) and www.china.org.cn (for a summary of China's political system and backgrounds of political leaders). Forbes Global compiled a list of the fifty richest entrepreneurs in China, who are estimated to be worth $200 million each. More information can be found on www.forbes.com/global/2000. For an English-language investment guide to China, www.fdi.gov.cn provides a user-friendly and authoritative source of information.

DOING BUSINESS IN CHINA

Establishing Your Credibility

Many women identify gender barriers to conducting business in China, though some find the problem less daunting than in Japan or Korea. The bright side is that most agree gender barriers can be overcome by demonstrating one's abilities. Individual competence, mutual trust, and product and service quality can all contribute to your credibility as a businesswoman. To establish credibility, women have to work doubly hard to be technically prepared and culturally astute.

CHALLENGES FOR WOMEN EXECUTIVES

In general, you can expect your Chinese counterparts to respond more to the men than to the women on your team. This is not surprising given the common assumption that men are more senior or knowledgeable than women. In fact, foreign businesswomen are relatively rare in China. Hence, women have complained of being uncomfortably noticed. It is all the harder in such situations for women executives to lead their team.

A female team leader can face problems establishing her credibility with the Chinese unless team members defer to her as the authoritative figure on the team. American men need to be aware that their tendency to jump in and answer questions, especially when a woman is speaking, undermines her authority and the team's effectiveness. Women should advise team members not to answer questions directed to her, but rather to defer to her whenever appropriate. A good response to a question that should be directed to a female colleague is: "Jane is the best person to answer that question." It is also helpful to make seating arrangements that will place the female manager in a position of authority.

> ### Uncomfortably Noticed
>
> "You are noticed, sometimes uncomfortably, as the Chinese are not used to a woman executive in many places where I conduct business. Some found it rather disturbing. For me, it was outright disruptive. I confirmed this with other female executives that I know in my industry who travel often to China. They had the same feeling of being noticed and observed." (San Jose, California)

ROLE OF THE SENIOR MANAGER

Senior managers play an important role in helping their female colleagues establish credibility in China. As a woman, you should advise management that your personal credibility may be jeopardized if your role is undermined, and that this could hinder the success of follow-up meetings.

Before negotiations, the manager can introduce female

staff members and highlight their expertise and achievements. During negotiations, the manager can act as a moderator who refers questions to the appropriate team member. For example, if a woman is not receiving due respect, the manager can bring attention to her role and authority.

MORE TIPS FOR ESTABLISHING CREDIBILITY

- Be visible. Attend and host meetings between your company and your Chinese counterparts whenever possible. Typically, it is the key decision-makers who take part in international travel and meetings, so being present adds to your credibility.
- Make sure the title on your business card clearly communicates your position. It is important that your counterpart understands where you fall in the hierarchy. If there is any doubt about your position, it may be assumed that you have a lesser role than other members on your team.
- If someone appears confused about your name and rank, offer another business card, even if you have already presented one. This is a subtle way of reinforcing your title and ensuring acknowledgment of your participation as an active member of the meeting
- Women should lead business discussions where possible. If there is only one woman and everyone is of equal rank, let the woman take the lead to help establish her credibility.

Business Meetings in China

ESTABLISH CONNECTIONS
Establish a network of personal connections on both official

and personal levels. Carefully cultivate them through regular contact. As Professor Ming-Jer Chen points out, relationships in China are cultivated through small but consistent gestures of friendship, such as making phone calls or paying short visits.[20] Consistency can reap big rewards, since the system is set up to serve the most familiar and most trusted partner first. Women can and should develop multilayered relationships with their Chinese contacts. Some women interviewed said that they also tried to develop relationships with their associates' colleagues, partners, and even family members, as these connections can become valuable assets in their business dealings. In China, who you know in addition to what you know is very important.

Here are some additional tips on establishing connections:

- Personal networks are important when working in China. Be prepared to spend considerable time socializing and networking when you are there.
- Make it a point to learn some Mandarin. It helps you to connect much more easily with your counterparts, as you will be seen more as an insider than a foreigner. If you can speak a few words of the local dialect, that would be even more appreciated.
- Do not cold call in China. If you are establishing business for the first time, use a third-party agent to help set up an initial meeting. You can secure one through your local consulate or business organizations.
- Companies should consider hiring someone to join the team who can understand both Chinese and Western business culture and operations. This is important to establishing long-term business in China.

INTRODUCTIONS

Introductions are important, particularly for women. If you

are doing business with a firm for the first time, have a higher-ranking person from your company, preferably someone who already knows your counterpart, introduce you. For newcomers, particularly women, this is the best way to present your credentials. By having a superior introduce you, it will also be easier for you to forge a relationship with your counterparts, as you will not be a total stranger to them. If an introduction cannot be done in advance in person, it can be handled by phone or e-mail. You may also bring with you written introductions from one or more people who are known and respected in China. Your biography should include your education, business expertise, and achievements.

> ### *Female Executives in China*
> "Compared to American female executives, who are far more assertive, women managers in China have to manage things from 'behind the scenes.' In China the role women play in business seems to be more administrative than managerial. For example, I have yet to meet a female VP from China coming to the U.S. but many female VPs from the U.S. travel to China."
> (San Francisco, California)

When you are introduced at the first meeting, state your credentials. Overemphasizing your credentials, however, is considered impolite. Women must strike a delicate balance to assert confidence yet avoid being seen as overbearing. Hence, while you should introduce your position in the firm, it is more appropriate to have your colleagues highlight your achievements. As discussed in Chapter 6, being modest (*keqi*) is an important part of Chinese decorum. Below are more tips on introduction.

- When you are introducing visiting senior and junior executives, introduce the senior executives first, and then the subordinates according to rank.
- When you are meeting someone whom you've met before

but who may not remember you, state your name and title first to avoid any embarrassment on his or her part.

- When you introduce a Chinese visitor to your firm's executives, state his or her name, title, and company, in that order.

GREETINGS

Handshakes are now a common form of business greeting in China, although some Chinese may still bow as a form of greeting, mostly to individuals of high status. Women should initiate a handshake if one is not offered. Oftentimes, Chinese men are unsure about how to approach foreign businesswomen and will wait for the woman to extend her hand first. The handshake is usually not as firm a grasp as in the West but a light, polite shake.

BUSINESS CARDS

As mentioned in Chapter 1, be prepared to bring plenty of business cards with you. As many as fifty cards may be handed out during a Chinese business session. In China, be mindful of the business card exchange procedure. Americans tend to be informal in their card exchange, while the Chinese view the exchange with a great deal of respect. Business cards are accepted and presented with both hands and with the title facing your counterpart. Read the business card carefully when it is handed to you. Hold on to the card instead of shoving it into a pocket or purse. Place the card in front of you at the meeting table for easy reference. Make notes on a piece of paper, not on the card, as this could be viewed as defacing the card, which is very disrespectful.

BUSINESS HOURS

The workweek is Monday through Friday. Normal working

hours are from 8 A.M. to 5 P.M. with a one-hour lunch break. Government offices, schools, and other institutions do not work on Saturday and Sunday. Hospitals, post offices, banks, monuments, and museums are usually open seven days a week from 8:30 or 9:00 A.M. to 6:00 P.M. Hospital emergency clinics are open even when the rest of the hospital is closed to visitors. Shops usually remain open from 8:30 or 9:00 A.M. to 8 P.M. every day, including public holidays. Restaurants and bars stay open later at night. It is possible to eat as late as 10:00 P.M., and some open-air restaurants even stay open into the late hours of the night. Opening hours may vary depending on the specific location.

> ### Hey, I'm Not the Interpreter!
> "On one of my initial trips, I traveled with my colleague who is an American male. So there were some from the Chinese side who initially thought I was his interpreter. I had to clear this up immediately. You can and need to do this immediately within the first three to four minutes as soon as you get there. You state who you are and what your expertise is and move on." (Chicago, Illinois)

PUNCTUALITY

Be on time for business meetings. In China, punctuality is often considered a reflection of your interest and sincerity. In major Chinese cities, you should take into consideration traffic congestion, so plan ahead and try to arrive early or on time. While your Chinese counterparts may be late for the meeting, it doesn't hurt for you to be punctual.

AGENDA

Your Chinese hosts will organize meetings from start to finish, from introductions to seating order, format, meals, content of discussion, and so forth. They try to ensure that the meeting will go smoothly and that there will be no surprises. As noted in Chapter 1, providing an agenda before the meeting can help guide the discussion and keep it from straying off track. Without a proper agenda, lengthy delays may result, as your counterparts would need to seek approval before making decisions.

At the meeting, the Chinese prefer to follow a given agenda, with hierarchical team roles and designations of a time for each person to speak. Decisions have usually been made before the meeting and any changes are discussed off-line. Common features of American meetings, such as brainstorming, free association, and exploratory communication, appear disorganized to the Chinese. If you have ideas, share them in private sessions, preferably with the key negotiator, either before or after the meeting and during breaks.

PARTICIPANTS

Americans tend to send one or two people to business meetings, and this small group is expected to take responsibility for the discussions and to make decisions. Often, one or two representatives are prepared to present terms and conditions to close a deal with the other side. The Chinese, on the other hand, will bring many people to business meetings. Colleagues who are adept in various fields of expertise will be asked to come on board so that all information is directly at hand. It is very difficult for the Chinese to understand how one person could be knowledgeable enough to represent all corporate disciplines and answer all questions. Americans likewise wonder how the Chinese can afford to send so many staff members and allow them to take so much time. When attending meetings with the Chinese, be prepared that you may be one small group dealing with a large number of participants on the other side of the table.

SEATING

In many cultures, seating arrangements at the business table and the sequence of entry into and exit from the room reflect hierarchical relationships. In China, the head executive will enter the room first, followed by an interpreter and staff members. As a general rule, the speakers for each group sit at the center of the conference table facing each other with their staff members seated around them in descending rank. The highest-ranking person will start the meeting and do most of the talking.

If you are confused about the seating arrangements, take your cue from your hosts and note where they are seated in order to locate your seat. If you are hosting a meeting, ask your Chinese colleagues to provide you with a list of the attendees and their rank in the organization. While some recommend using place cards to help each person find his or her seat, it is usually easier for you as host to indicate where your guests are to be seated. Female managers in particular should pay attention to seating protocols so that you don't end up sitting at a place designated for lower-ranking staff members.

> ### *Lost in Translation*
>
> "Our contract was in English. They said they needed the Chinese-language contract. They offered to translate the letter of intent, which we agreed to. But I had someone else translate it back to me to make sure it was the same as the English version, and we were shocked to learn it was different. So I had to politely confront them and ask that they match the English version. We lost trust at that point." (Boston, Massachusetts)

INTERPRETERS

If you decide that you need an interpreter or translator, be sure you get one who is familiar with the technical terms used in your industry. If you will be negotiating legal contracts, it is helpful to engage a bilingual lawyer. Try to hire an interpreter who has been recommended by other American firms rather than one recommended by the company with whom you are planning to do business. Spend some time with the interpreter reviewing the proposed agenda, negotiation content, technical material, and your expectations. Avoid using jargon or slang that your interpreter is not likely to be familiar with. Make short statements so that they are more accurately translated. While using an interpreter can facilitate communication, expect the meeting to be lengthened threefold as a result.

> ### *Countering Prejudice*
>
> "Chinese men have the same prejudice against businesswomen as North American and European men. Chinese customers see us as inferior to our male counterparts, and that takes some time to overcome. I feel the best way to overcome these issues is to demonstrate your ability and credibility." (Expatriate, Hong Kong)

PRESENTATIONS

Handouts and visual aids will enhance your presentation and make it easier to understand. Charts outlining each major point are well received. Presentations should be brief. Offer solid facts with documented sources in a friendly, low-key but persuasive manner. Translate all materials and provide handouts to ensure that your presentation is understood. Allow time for questions.

BREAKS

If you are holding a daylong meeting, your host will probably arrange for at least one break in the morning and afternoon. In China, breaks are the best time for one-on-one informal negotiations with your counterparts, especially on sensitive issues that cannot be raised openly at large meetings. If you are hosting the meeting, have cold drinks, coffee, tea, and light snacks available. Also provide a separate room for your counterparts in case they need to discuss among themselves.

MEALS

Meals are an important part of doing business in China. Allow time for meals with your Chinese counterparts, whether you are a guest or host. The business dinner, in particular, is a critical extension of the business meeting. Businesspeople are expected to accept dinner invitations when on business in China and to host dinners when they are receiving Chinese guests. Women should be sure to attend business dinners and consider them part of the business day. Do not bow out. Wining and dining etiquette is discussed in more detail in Chapter 8.

6

NEGOTIATING IN CHINA

Inside Chinese Negotiation

There has been ample research on Chinese negotiation style by Lucian Pye, Nancy Adler, Rosalie Tung, Tony Fang, and Scott Seligman, to name a few. In general, most authors suggest that the Chinese have a unique negotiating style that is skillful, tough, shrewd, and tenacious. Some have described the Chinese as win-lose negotiators, and others as win-win, or honest at one moment and dishonest at another.[21] Lucian Pye suggests that because Chinese society is changing so rapidly, we cannot look to any one system or formula for negotiations, as negotiation styles will be constantly evolving.[22]

Chinese use a variety of tactics at the negotiation table. Tony Fang[23] has identified two major influences behind the tactics used in Chinese negotiations. The first hails from the Chinese bureaucracy school, which believes that Chinese negotiation style is forged by the political institutions and culture of the communist government. Business negotiators, many of whom are state officials, fear criticism, avoid responsibility, and show indecision in the negotiation process. Ambiguity and delay are the most commonly employed tactics. Oftentimes, the negotiation comes across as scripted and rehearsed when key decision makers are not present.

The second influence comes from the Confucian school, in which business negotiations are conducted according to reciprocal relationships. Confucians view the world in terms of the five cardinal relationships: ruler and minister, father and son, husband and wife, elder and younger brothers, and friends. All relationships are defined in terms of reciprocity, that is, if you are good to me, I will be good to you. This style of negotiation is marked by an emphasis on trust, saving face, moral cultivation and harmony. Many of the tactics are tuned toward testing one's trustworthiness and commitment to sustaining a long-term relationship.

According to Fang, we can look to some key concepts in Chinese philosophy and culture to help understand and become more effective in negotiations with the Chinese: *guanxi, renqing, li,* and *keqi.*

GUANXI

Fang defines *guanxi* as "personal contacts or connections." Seligman describes it as reciprocal obligation that individuals have to each other for which they can make unlimited demands.[24] Pye describes it as a friendship with the continual exchange of favors.[25] To succeed in the Chinese market, it is essential to build a *guanxi* network of colleagues, business associates, friends, and family members, who can help to get things done. However, in their study of firms doing business in China, Yeung and Tung find *guanxi* to be a necessary but insufficient condition for long-term business,[26] for while it is important to develop *guanxi* networks, it is just as important to pay attention to the quality of your goods and services.

RENQING

Fang defines *renqing* as "human feelings." More specifically, it can refer to feelings of gratitude and/or a principle of reciprocating favors. Common Chinese expressions include giving someone a favor (*song renqing*) and owing someone a favor (*qian renqing*). As a Chinese interviewee recalled, "I remember my parents always counting favors with their friends and business colleagues, as to whom they owed and who owed them. *Renqing* was exchanged in numerous ways: gifts, wedding, recommendations, etc. I think you have to be aware of *renqing*. That is, when you ask people for a favor, they will expect something back eventually and it may be expected during negotiations."

> ### Saving Face
>
> "I have worked with Chinese governments. I find the concept of saving face and letting them think that it is their idea is very important. I recall we had a delegation, and we wanted a boat reception for them. Our local office advised us that they would not be interested in this unless they suggested it. So we had to ask, 'We have a group of visitors and we want to show off the city. What is the best way to do that?' To which they suggested a boat reception. And everything worked out fine." (Sacramento, California)

LI

Fang defines *li* as rules of conduct, etiquette, and politeness. *Li* are the norms of propriety through which the Chinese position themselves and perform their roles according to the social hierarchy. *Li* composes the standards of how human interactions are conducted. The concept of gift giving relates to *li*. Even simple acts like how seating arrangements are made also constitute *li*.

KEQI

Keqi is part of *li*. Fang defines *keqi* literally as the appropriate behavior of a guest. It describes a combination of qualities, including modesty, courtesy, and consideration of others. This concept is perhaps the most elusive to Americans, who are typically forthright and direct. For example, when invited to a dinner, a Chinese may decline the offer rhetorically by claiming that he does not wish to impose upon the host. The host may then reply, "*Bu yong keqi*" (don't be modest), and with a little tug-of-war of gentle words, the dinner invitation is finally accepted.

GENERAL TIPS ON NEGOTIATING IN CHINA

- Gather information in advance. This can be done by making a number of visits to the firm and meeting people.
- Use the first meeting to build your relationship and establish a working rapport. It is best not to launch directly into your business proposal.
- Remember that saving face and reciprocating favors are important concepts in China. Avoid confrontational communication and try to give and take.
- Instead of asking yes/no questions, ask open-ended questions that will initiate dialogue.
- Observe body language closely, as you may be able to spot nonverbal clues that indicate they do not agree with a point. A "yes" response or a smile can mean only "I hear and understand you." Clarify what their position is.
- Do not push for a decision on the spot. Your Chinese associate will have to consult with their superiors before they can make a decision. Pushing will cause them to lose face.
- Listen actively. You will be more effective if you listen and question the Chinese participants rather than simply respond to them.

The Negotiation Process

Most researchers differentiate five distinct steps in the negotiating process: preparation, relationship building, information exchange, persuasion, and finally, agreement. In international negotiations, the process of negotiation is the same, but preparation must involve learning about and understanding the culture of your counterparts. More specifically, the negotiation stages are as follows:

- The preparation stage takes place before you go on your trip to meet your counterparts. During this phase, it is important that you meet with your team, clarify your aims and the positions that you will take, and define each participant's role. It is very helpful to role-play the scenarios that might occur during international negotiations. Conduct research on the business culture and environment in China. Plan the logistics of the meeting ahead of time.

- The relationship stage will start when the two teams or parties meet and get to know each other. Lunches, dinners, and informal conversations are the best occasions for building a personal relationship. Both parties at this stage seek to identify common areas of interest and establish rapport.

- The information stage occurs at the meeting table. Company exchanges of information on services, products, and proposals are presented formally. Question-and-answer sessions take place.

- Persuasion begins after the proposals are delivered, and differences between the parties become clear. At this stage, each party strives to present his or her position and to persuade the other party to compromise on a solution.

- The final agreement stage is when both parties come to a mutually acceptable position. Western cultures tend to view the signing of the contract as the final step; with the Chinese, it is the commencement of business or even the receipt of the final payment.

> *Preparing to Negotiate*
>
> "Negotiating in China? The Chinese have a totally different mentality from Americans. How do you prepare for that kind of negotiation? It is about finding the right people and striking the right relationship." (New York, New York)

Cultural differences are likely to occur at every stage and will become more pronounced as the negotiation proceeds. In China, be prepared for long negotiations and to negotiate even after the agreement is signed, as cultural differences will persist even during the implementation of the agreement.

Comparing Negotiation Culture and Style

Clearly, the type of culture in which businesspeople operate has an impact on cross-cultural communications and relationships. According to Cohen, culture greatly impacts how particular groups of businesspeople negotiate.[27] It is therefore important to identify different types of negotiation culture and style before venturing to the negotiation table.

NEGOTIATING WITH HIGH-CONTEXT CULTURES

China can be identified as a "high-context culture." A high-context negotiator's focus is to not lose face, and he or she will do everything in order to ensure that harmony is maintained on the surface. A high-context negotiator will also strive to take as much uncertainty out of the situation as possible, so that there will be no surprises. A failure to reach an agreement can result in a loss of face.

> ### Negotiating with Friends
> "I think the key to negotiating with the Chinese is to establish a relationship before you start to negotiate. It is easier to work with friends than with strangers. They asked us how we rated next to our competitors. We were ready to be honest about it. We wanted to teach them why they ought to do business with us." (Detroit, Michigan)

In his research, Cohen compares China and Japan as two different examples of high-context cultures. He finds that the Japanese will conduct extensive information gathering so they can estimate the other party's position and then adjust their own position to reach a compromise. Averting a stalemate at the negotiating table is part of their efforts to save face. The Chinese negotiators, on the other hand, will take a slightly different approach. They will make sure that the other party is aware of the non-negotiable positions and will only come to the table if these terms have been implicitly accepted. They will not come to the table if they think there is potential for conflict and humiliation. The common denominator between these two positions, according to Cohen, is "avoiding a leap into the unknown," that is, to reduce uncertainties and the potential for loss of face.

NEGOTIATING WITH POLYCHRONIC CULTURES

When Mao Zedong was asked what he thought of the French Revolution, he replied, "It is too soon to tell." Unlike Americans, who tend to focus on quick results, the Chinese prefer to take their time. To them, time is cyclical rather than linear. The concept of polychronic/monochronic cultures has been introduced by E. T. Hall. In polychronic cultures, multiple tasks are handled at the same time, and time is less important than interpersonal relations. Producing a satisfactory agreement as soon as possible may be one of the least important concerns for the Chinese. Instead, they believe that a considerable amount of time should be invested in establishing a climate of trust and understanding and in matters quite apart from the issues brought to the negotiating table. Your Chinese counterparts tend not to view time as a constraint or as a set of limits in which a particular task must be completed.

Negotiations are smoother when there is trust between parties. The longer the relationship is in place, the more say you have during negotiations. Matching favors is an important part of the negotiation process, and you should try to keep track of the gives and takes. Some women found negotiating with government officials more difficult than with private business people, as negotiations were wrapped up in cumbersome protocol. Nothing was straightforward. Most women remarked that the terms of contracts have much less meaning to the Chinese than the actual process of resolving conflicts.

AMERICAN NEGOTIATING STYLE

Americans tend to question and challenge at business meetings. We want to brainstorm at the table to find creative solutions. We are quick to jump into a business discussion and stay at it long into dinner and afterward. We tend to be task-oriented, adopting a direct and sometimes confrontational communication style. Americans usually operate under time pressure, which leads to impatience during protracted business meetings. In general, we approach a meeting with targets and deadlines. We assume that one individual is authorized to have full control of the decision-making process at the table.

When Americans make an agreement, it is usually the value of the deal that makes it attractive to them. Americans are less concerned about whom they buy their products and services from, and are more concerned with cost, features, and value for money. Most significantly, Americans value the rule of law. Contracts are seen as binding and parties are expected to adhere strictly to the terms.

CHINESE NEGOTIATING STYLE

Chinese use the business meeting for information gathering, presenting ideas, and developing consensus. Much of the material they want to cover at the meeting can therefore seem intrusive to the American business executive. While the business concept of privacy is growing in China, it still does not meet American expectations. Many Chinese firms like to know everything about the operations of your business and the competition faced in the industry. Hence, they may ask you questions that you do not wish to answer. Try to deal with these questions tactfully without causing a loss of face. These questions are actually efforts by your Chinese associates to get to know you and the industry better. It is important for the Chinese to trust people with whom they partner before the technicalities of products and services are taken into consideration.

The Chinese prefer not to make decisions at the negotiation table. This is done in between or after meetings. It is customary for them to informally drop hints and make inquiries outside of the meeting during breaks and in the evening. When things are not going well, they may deliberately delay proceedings through a variety of tactics rather than admit that the discussion has hit a stalemate. They may even report that things are going well when they are not. You must therefore exercise caution before accepting what your Chinese partners say at face value.

Furthermore, a contract is not seen as the end of the negotiations. It is just the beginning of a relationship that will change continuously as it is reevaluated and renegotiated. Frequently, it is after the agreement is signed that problems arise.

In their desire to create harmony, Chinese may give answers they believe Americans want to hear, rather than true answers. This can prevent you from obtaining a realistic picture of what is going on and lead you to assume that the deal has come to closure. Complications arise when you proceed as if the deal has been closed and the Chinese continue to explore areas for compromise. A savvy businesswoman will therefore continue to assess whether every aspect of the business discussion has been accepted to ensure that both sides are comfortable with each point of the agreement before moving on to the next.

> ### Title Conscious
> "I work for a high-profile university and we were at the point of signing a contract with a Chinese firm for some of our courses. I learned that matching titles were very important for the Chinese. We had a letter of intent that indicated our titles. To match ours, they changed their titles and even the name of the institution to match us. It was all made up. Our concern became: were they empowered to sign?" (Boston, Massachusetts)

Modifying Your Negotiation Style

When negotiating with the Chinese, you will need to adjust your style of negotiation. For most Americans, this means being more patient. Negotiations with the Chinese tend to be protracted by American standards. Disregarding organizational hierarchy and demanding decisions to be made quickly will only prolong the negotiations. Instead, you should try to operate within the Chinese system and frame of mind. Pay attention to informal discussions, and use your *guanxi* network to resolve problems that are otherwise intractable at the negotiation table.

With an emphasis on preserving harmony, the Chinese try to avoid overt conflict. So they will often smile and nod even when they do not agree with or understand you. Hence, American-style frankness is not appreciated. Be subtle when you speak and become attuned to the nuances of what your Chinese counterparts say. Since preserving face is critical in China, be generous with praise but tactful with criticisms.

Caution: Kickbacks

"When I go to China, I tend to use a straightforward American style because I have lived in the U.S. for so long. There are ethical issues in China, like kickbacks and under-the-table deals. Since I represented an American company, I did not participate in such activities." (Los Angeles, California)

When speaking, try to tone down your voice, as loudness can be interpreted as aggression or anger. Also refrain from any open displays of emotions, which are viewed as a loss of self-control. Westerners tend to have bold facial expressions and body gestures that can be unsettling to their counterparts. As best as possible, keep your composure.

One executive even described how she had to calibrate the group dynamics of her Chinese counterparts in order to maintain a harmonious atmosphere: "I was negotiating with a senior manager in China who had one idea but his staff another. If I took either one of the two views, I would create a situation where one or the other would lose face. So instead I tried to reach a compromise proposal. If you embarrass someone you discredit yourself as much as you discredit him or her. You have to be very careful how you act and say things even if there are mistakes made. Do not assign blame. Do not humiliate anyone."

In general, work with your Chinese counterparts, not against them. Focus your negotiations on how both of you can benefit. And finally, know your products and theirs, as well as the competition. Knowing your product line and understanding how it can fit into your counterpart's strategy will help strengthen your position. View negotiations as key to establishing and retaining a long-term relationship.

WOMEN IN NEGOTIATION

There has been significant research conducted on the differences in negotiating styles between women and men and the strengths and weaknesses of each. Most businesswomen I have studied reported that negotiating effectiveness in the international environment is based less on individual negotiating style than on perceptions of how each gender is supposed to behave in a foreign culture.[28]

When you enter into business negotiations with your international counterparts, it is important that you understand how they view women from their cultural perspective. A successful American businesswoman needs to understand not only how her international associates conduct business in general, but also the gender expectations that are part of the culture. For example, women may be expected to acquiesce rather than to be assertive, and this may impact the way a woman is received during business negotiations. Fortunately, most women report that initial, traditional expectations can easily be overcome if the negotiation is run effectively. Typically feminine attributes such as active listening, empathy, distinguishing between needs and positions, using collaborative language, and consensus seeking can help you forge common ground during negotiations.

In general, businesswomen advise that some of the best practices for women negotiating internationally include:

- Establish an environment of trust and foster open communication with your counterparts.
- Be well prepared for your meetings and negotiations;

identify and provide responses to possible points of contention in advance.

- Propose an agenda and try to keep the negotiation on course. Make clear the goals and alternatives.
- Adopt a collaborative and problem-solving attitude.
- Be well versed in the technical issues.

GENDER ISSUES IN CHINESE BUSINESS

Since ancient times, women have been viewed in most cultures as men's inferiors, physically, morally, and intellectually. In Western cultures today, women enjoy more freedom and equality than ever before.

Yet, despite gains made in recent years, particularly in the U.S., women's access to education, employment, health care, and political influence remains limited as societies worldwide maintain centuries-old social and religious laws, customs, and traditions that create barriers to equal rights for women.

For women doing business in China, gender inequality can prevent female managers from effectively performing their jobs. It is therefore important for American businesswomen working in China to be aware of gender issues such as harassment and discrimination that may arise.

Sexual Harassment

Sexual harassment is usually defined as a form of discrimination in which sexual advances or requests for sexual favors constitute a condition of a person's employment or advancement in the workplace. It frequently occurs between a male and a female, often instigated by a male manager or another male in power. While many countries have begun to enact laws against sexual harassment, it has been reported that often such laws are not effectively enforced.

Sexual harassment occurs in workplaces worldwide, including the United States. Laws that specifically prohibit sexual harassment have been passed in Argentina, Australia, Canada, France, Germany, Israel, Mexico, Netherlands, the U.K., and the U.S., but many other countries are still grappling with the problem or have not even recognized it as such. In China, the government has recently announced plans to enact the first anti–sexual harassment law.[29]

There are two types of sexual harassment defined by U.S. law: quid pro quo and hostile environment. "Quid pro quo" means that an employee is asked to perform a sexual act in exchange for a job, promotion, or other perks. A "hostile environment" is described as one that contains situations, acts, or items that can inhibit the productivity of a female employee, such as sexually suggestive language, behavior, or pictures.

Some strategies for employees who experience sexual harassment include confronting the harassing individual, notifying the management, or, should management be the offender, notifying the personnel department or the Equal Employment Opportunity Commission (EEOC). (In the United States, call toll-free 1-800-669-EEOC or see www.eeoc.gov to find your local office.) The EEOC will provide you with written guidelines to determine what constitute sexual harassment and how to deal with it.

Sexual Discrimination

The American businesswoman may unavoidably be party to conversations and actions that discriminate against women. For example, in an Asian context, it is natural to ask a female employee to serve tea. A woman may also be subjected to innocent questions about her age or marital status and whether or not she has children. In Korea and Japan, the norm is for men to enter rooms and elevators ahead of women. In Europe, office talk tends to be rather flirtatious, sprinkled with many off-color jokes and puns. Derogatory statements about women in Germany are often expressed openly in the office, and reference to a woman's physique is not uncommon in Italy and France.

Some women report that suggestive sexual comments are occasionally used (consciously or unconsciously) as negotiating tools to throw a woman off her guard. Women must be prepared for these tactics and to handle derogatory remarks calmly but assertively. Some tactics women have used to respond to such situations include politely reminding your counterparts that you are conducting a business session, suggesting a break and stating that the negotiation has gone off track, or ending the negotiation in its entirety to show absolute intolerance and disapproval.

GENDER PERCEPTIONS IN CHINA

In traditional Chinese society, males, who play the roles of rulers, protectors, cultivators, and breadwinners, are valued over females. According to an old Chinese saying, "Women are the moon reflecting the sunlight," that is, the role of women is merely to reflect the glow of men—the male works outside of the home to earn an income, while the female stays home to raise children and manage the household. Consequently, Chinese men have been dominant over Chinese women and have largely controlled their means of livelihood.

Many centuries ago, China's elite male philosophers developed precepts of social behavior that women were expected, or forced, to follow. Women were subordinated to their fathers, brothers, husbands, and even sons. Historically, marriages in China were arranged not for love, but for family connections. The bride usually lived under the dominion of her husband's mother and frequently faced competition from secondary wives and concubines. The husband was allowed to repudiate his wife, especially if she did not produce a male heir. If the husband died, the wife could not easily remarry. She had no economic independence, was frequently illiterate, and had no property rights. Infanticide resulted from parents not wishing to have female children.

Today, China maintains a strong patriarchal tradition. When a woman marries, she joins her husband's family, and ties with her own family may weaken. The couple either lives with the husband's family or, as is occurring more frequently, on their own. Divorce is considered shameful and is rarely discussed. If there is a divorce, the father often gets custody of the children.

However, modern Chinese women have become increasing assertive and economically independent. More and more women are joining the workforce, and some have risen to leadership positions in the government and private sector. Divorce rates, which used to be very low in China, are also growing. Young, educated Chinese women emphasize their individuality, independence, and hard work, and seek to pursue successful careers even as they try to maintain their femininity and family duties. Yet, recent studies on Chinese women indicate that many still feel inferior to men and worry about juggling career and family. Job discrimination is still widely practiced in China, and the stereotyping of women as the weaker sex persists.

Foreign women may face more obstacles than Chinese women in conducting business in China, because foreign, and in particular Western, women have to overcome both cultural and gender barriers. For example, foreign women have been dubbed "babes," and in local soap dramas, they are often portrayed as loose and flirtatious.[30]

STRATEGIES FOR COPING

It is important for you, your team, and your managers to know what strategies to pursue if you find yourself in a compromising situation. In cases where women have been harassed, managers should understand how to act in accordance with company policy and governing laws. It is important to realize, for example, that an executive team based in the home office in the United States is actually legally responsible for the actions of their employees worldwide, including in foreign subsidiaries.

Working internationally can be challenging. Many foreign countries have no laws or regulations concerning sexual harassment. But even if such laws are enacted, they are hard to enforce. Moreover, employees and partners in a country like China may not share the American viewpoint on gender issues. As a result, male managers in the U.S., who are unfamiliar with more traditional societies, may avoid sending female staff members to represent their companies, fearing that women cannot be effective in male-oriented societies. This assumption, however, keep these executives from using what is in fact their strongest asset—women—since typical feminine attributes, such as good listening, effective mediating, and consensus building, are well received in international business, and especially in non-confrontational business cultures. Male managers should inform themselves about the gender situation in other countries and what their responsibilities are in the event of sexual harassment, in order to send their female staff members to these countries with confidence.

U.S. courts (see www.eeoc.gov) offer some legal remedies and suggestions for handling discrimination and harassment situations: "The (U.S.) courts have established that corporations that assign a U.S. citizen to a post in a foreign country must treat that employee as if he or she were in the U.S., regardless of local customs and traditions." Recent Supreme Court cases have suggested several legal and human resource strategies to prevent gender discrimination. The first is "to educate and prepare employees sent to work in different countries abroad. Should a dispute arise, arbitration or mediation is preferred over litigation. The best overall strategy is to develop and implement a well-conceived company policy that ensures gender equality." [31]

MANAGEMENT RESPONSIBILITY

The elimination of sexual harassment starts at home. If your company does not have a policy on sexual discrimination and harassment, there will be little to back you up if you find yourself facing such situations in the international environment. Top management must therefore take a proactive role in enacting clear policies to eradicate harassment from the workplace. There are many good reasons for doing so. Sexual harassment can reduce employee productivity and morale, and consequently, have a negative impact on the company's bottom line. Even more significantly perhaps, sexual discrimination and harassment lawsuits can cost firms a great deal of financial and reputation losses.

It is the responsibility of the executive staff to eliminate sexual harassment. Top management must instruct its staff that sexual harassment is illegal and will not be tolerated. Issuing sexual harassment policies, scheduling open discussions, expressing disapproval, creating a path for complaint and resolution, and respecting individual privacy should all be part of the top management plan. A comfortable environment with open, company-wide communication is key to alleviating any inhibitions employees may have about revealing their experiences.

As a first step, a company needs a visible, comprehensive policy emphasizing the importance of appropriate behavior—harassment and social misconduct toward any employee will not be tolerated. This policy should also state the ramifications of any violation. Hard copies of the company policy should be distributed not only internally but also to customers and suppliers. A copy of the policy should be available to all employees and visibly posted in work and rest areas. The company should have training programs for its management staff and employees on a regular basis.

If you are in management, you can play a key role. Do not overlook or refuse to acknowledge problems that occur in other countries, because this will only reinforce acceptance toward inappropriate behavior. If one of your traveling staff is harassed, it will interfere with the productivity of your business dealings. Harassment also violates U.S. law. It is frustrating for a female worker facing sexual harassment to work with or for staff members who do not understand the seriousness of their offense, or to travel with managers who do not speak or act on behalf of the employee.

INDIVIDUAL RESPONSIBILITY

Prepare yourself for the possibility of encountering sexual harassment when you travel abroad. When you are visiting countries that have a limited awareness of women's rights, your actions can protect you from harassment more effectively than written policies. In these situations, men won't expect women to assert themselves, so if you strongly voice disapproval of inappropriate behavior, the offenders will often back down. Most businessmen would not want to lose a deal by offending a female associate.

Most women report that while their business days go smoothly, after-hours socializing can become a challenge. It is common, for example, for Chinese men to go out drinking after work. While drinking, they feel more comfortable chatting and becoming friendly. If you are the lone woman in your group, you may become the target for questions that would not usually be asked during office hours. In China, drinking can become an excuse for what Americans consider appallingly inappropriate behavior. While the American businesswomen may remain upset about an untoward incident or remark that happened the previous evening, the Chinese participants would probably ignore the offense the next day as they carry on with business as usual.

Should you be subjected to what you feel is sexual harassment, remain calm and professional. This attitude will have much more impact than if you become upset or angry. In many cases, men may have been trying to incite you or test your resilience. In most cases, you can either respond with a calm statement of disapproval, or show your disapproval by remaining silent. If you are in a situation that has become particularly unpleasant, you can always leave.

If you are traveling overseas on business and have been harassed, you are still protected as an employee of a U.S. firm and should take action in accordance with your firm's sexual harassment policy. It is always best to report the incident rather than to keep it to yourself. This way, if the perpetrator is an employee of your firm, he can be corrected or reprimanded, and if he is employed by another firm, at least your executives will be aware of the issue when deciding whether to enter into further business dealings with that company.

- If you are single, avoid talking about your personal life or dating, as these subjects can lead to uncomfortable conversations. In particular, do not mention that you are divorced or unmarried and living with a partner.
- If you feel that a conversation is inappropriate, don't respond. Just change the subject.
- Avoid situations where any unwanted intimacy may be initiated, such as dinners for two.
- Be careful that your actions cannot be interpreted as being either aggressive or flirtatious.
- If your international hosts insist on opening doors for you or holding your chair at the dining table, graciously allow them to do so. Remember they are trying to respond appropriately when working with women.
- Avoid eating or drinking alone in strange restaurants, since you may be viewed as a pick-up target. Ask your hotel concierge for restaurant recommendations.

RESPONDING TO UNCOMFORTABLE QUESTIONS

When you are asked a question you consider uncomfortable or inappropriate, use short, standard answers to discourage further questioning. For example, many women are asked about their marital status, age, children, etc. While these questions may seem unusual, they are often commonly asked in foreign countries as a way of expressing interest about you. You can answer these in a polite, vague manner, such as "My career keeps me very busy" or "I am younger than I look." You can also choose to ignore the question and change the subject to redirect the conversation. If the questions are more direct and sexual in nature, be assertive and answer, "This is not an appropriate question to ask," or, if the questioner continues to be uncooperative, try to embarrass him by telling another group member about your discomfort. Silence can also be very effective.

Strategies for responding to uncomfortable questions also include:

- You may be asked seemingly intrusive questions about your marital status and whether or not you have children. Prepare some stock answers or change the topic of conversation to one that is more comfortable for you.
- You might be invited to a bar after dinner. Whether or not you want to attend is your choice. It's not impolite to say no, giving jet lag or business commitments such as faxes, e-mails, or phone calls as an excuse.
- If your host exhibits inappropriate behavior, inform him that you are uncomfortable and that you want him to stop.
- If you are traveling with a team, have other team members join you in expressing dissatisfaction with the situation. This will usually end the unwanted behavior, since to continue will cause bad feelings.
- If you are in a social setting that is becoming uncomfortable, inform your host that you are uncomfortable and would like to leave. Politely request that he call you a taxi. If he does not cooperate, ask the establishment's staff to call one for you.
- If no action is taken, get ready to leave and state the reasons you are leaving. There is no reason to stay in a situation that is uncomfortable for you.
- If you want to leave while your colleagues desire to stay, you should do so and not feel bad about "breaking up the fun."

8

DINING, FOOD, AND HOSTING IN CHINA

Dining in China

Dining is part and parcel of doing business in China. Entertaining is done outside the home. You will be invited to attend lunches and dinners during your stay. It is important that you participate in these social meals because dining is an extension of the business meeting and is crucial to relationship building. The more relaxed the dining atmosphere, the more you can build rapport with your Chinese business peers.

In China, businesspeople are expected to accept dinner invitations and to host dinners when they are receiving international guests. Turning down a business dinner can mean a lack of interest or that you are not an important member of the business team. In return, plan to host and participate in lunches and dinners when your Chinese partners visit you.

Business meals are times to relax and enjoy good food. Dining conversations provide opportunities for you to learn more about your counterparts and vice versa, and to build a more personal relationship. As a rule, avoid raising controversial subjects, such as Taiwan's independence or the Japanese occupation, and do not discuss business issues unless your Chinese associates do. Instead, try to inquire about interesting local topics, such as culture, food, sights, and so on.

The Joy of Eating

"The Chinese love to eat. Eating is an excellent way to connect with your counterparts. They get to know you personally over a meal, more so than Americans do. Don't dive into business during the first lunch or dinner; you need to warm up to this. Just use the dining time to establish rapport and trust." (Chicago, Illinois)

While it is meant to be fun and relaxing, business dining in China can present a few challenges to American businesspeople. Long, formal dinners with many courses (as many as eight to sixteen) are common, a tedious activity for those who would rather retreat to their hotel rooms after a long day of work. You may also be introduced to new and sometimes unusual foods that you may balk at eating. The Chinese are furthermore avid drinkers, and even women are asked to participate in drinking. The American businesswomen should therefore be prepared for what to expect when dining in China.

Dining Etiquette

At restaurants, Chinese tables are round and usually have a rotating server (like a lazy Susan) in the center. Your place setting will include a plate, soup bowl, chopsticks on a rest, and spoon.

Communal serving utensils (e.g., a ladle for soup or a pair of serving chopsticks) are usually provided for shared dishes. If they aren't provided, it is good manners to turn your chopsticks around and use the gripping ends to transfer food onto your plate. Instead of a napkin, you may be given a damp cloth to clean your hands before and after your meal. It is not intended for your face. Since few restaurants provide napkins, it is wise to carry a handkerchief, tissues, or towelettes with you.

SERVING FOOD AND BEVERAGES

In China, food is shared. Each diner, who is provided with her own plate and bowl, takes food from the shared dishes on the server and then rotates it to the next person. There can be up to sixteen courses for formal dinners, usually served one dish at a time, and as few as four courses for a simple lunch, generally served at the same time. Unlike in the West, where you are served a whole plate at a time, Chinese will take one piece from the main dish to their plate and eat it before reaching for the next piece. Most do not wait for all to be served before starting to eat, although you should wait for the host to start. He or she will enthusiastically urge the guests to tuck into the food.

At a typical meal, appetizers such as pickles, vegetables, peanuts, or crackers will be served first, followed by cold

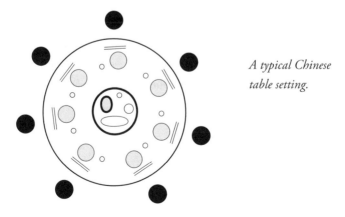

A typical Chinese table setting.

dishes, hot dishes, soup, and finally dessert. The host will order enough dishes, and oftentimes too many, to make sure that no one leaves the meal hungry. Rice or noodles may not be served unless you ask for them. Noodles are usually preferred to rice in Northern China, and rice is preferred in Southern China. Some hosts do not view rice or noodles as appropriate for guest dining but rather as a staple for domestic dining. There will be a number of dipping sauces served with each meal. Some sauces are for specific dishes. If you are unsure which sauce should be matched with which dish, don't be shy to ask your host.

Seafood may be served, which is significant, as it is expensive (equivalent to serving filet mignon in the West.) In addition to fish, seafood dishes may include squid, scallops, and sea cucumber. A whole fish or chicken may be served that will include the head, tail, fins, and feet, which signifies that the food is fresh and that no parts have been removed. The Chinese relish eating all parts of the fish or chicken, including chicken liver, heart, neck, feet, and even the eyes of the fish. In the chicken, the leg is considered the tastiest piece, and this might be offered to the guest as a sign of hospitality. In the fish, the cheek is the tenderest part.

For beverage, tea is served during the meal, and there are a variety of choices, the most popular of which include Jupu, Teiguanyin, and Longjin. In most restaurants, sodas like Coke and Seven Up are also readily available. Last but not least, alcohol will not be missed. The Chinese usually serve wine and beer. Traditionally brewed wines like Shaoxing (rice wine) and Gaoliang (sorghum wine) have alcohol content as high as 60 percent, so be prepared!

Drinking and Preparing Tea

In most parts of China the tea is served in small clay teapots. The process of preparing tea is an elaborate art known as *cha dao* (which literally means "the way of tea"). The pot is rinsed with boiling water, and then the leaves are added. The tea leaves are first rinsed in hot water in the pot, before more hot water is added to make the tea. Teacups are arranged in a circle, and after a minute of brewing, the tea is poured into the cups. The cups are filled to just over the halfway point to signal that the rest of the cup is filled with friendship and affection. The server will pass the tea to guests and invite them to smell the fragrance of the tea.

You might notice that the Chinese tap their fingers three times when tea is being poured. It is a silent expression of gratitude to the server. The story dates back to the Qing Dynasty, when one of the emperors went out in disguise on inspection

---

More on Chinese Tea

Tea is the most common beverage in China. It is said that tea originated there as early as A.D. 300. Legend has it that an emperor discovered tea when leaves accidentally blew into the water he was boiling. When he went to throw it out, he noticed a fragrant smell emanating from the liquid, and out of curiosity, he tasted the brew. Pleased by his new discovery, he shared it with his people.

The Chinese were the first to cultivate the tea plant, *camellia sinensis*, from which all true teas are said to originate. The Chinese were also the first to develop the Yixing teapot, an unglazed lead-free small pot.

In ancient China, tea was used for medicinal purposes. Modern research suggests that tea does indeed have many qualities for promoting good health.

Green tea is sometimes referred to as "true" tea, which has undergone minimal oxidation. It is popular in China and Japan and in recent years has become increasingly popular in the West.

Oolong tea is a traditional Chinese tea and is somewhere between green and black tea in terms of the oxidation process. The tea produces a strong brew and has a bitter aftertaste. Oolong tea is the type of tea most commonly served in Chinese restaurants.

Black tea is also referred to as a "true" tea, but the leaves are more heavily oxidized than the green and oolong varieties. Black tea is generally stronger in flavor and contains more caffeine than the more lightly oxidized teas. Black tea is also referred to as red tea in China because of the color of the liquid.

trips to South China. When the emperor poured tea for his companions, they felt compelled to bow to him for the great honor that he was bestowing on them. In an effort to conceal his identity, the emperor told them to tap the table three times with their fingers instead of bowing.

There are several special circumstances in which tea is prepared and consumed. In Chinese society, the younger generation shows respect to the older generation by offering a cup of tea. Tea drinking in restaurants is an important family activity for special gatherings. In the past, people of lower rank served tea to people of higher rank. While this rule has relaxed somewhat, in formal business situations the lower-ranking person should not expect the higher-ranking person to serve tea.

> ### Unusual Fare
>
> "There was an exotic-food restaurant at my hotel. It served rat, dog, snake, etc. I took a photo of the menu to prove it. I asked a Chinese colleague about it and she said, 'In China we eat everything that has legs except the table, and everything that flies except an airplane.' After that I looked at all my food very carefully." (Long Island, New York)

USING CHOPSTICKS

Chopsticks in China are long and thin. Use the ends you grasp with for communal serving (picking up items to your plate) and the pointed ends for personal eating. If you are very uncomfortable with using chopsticks, you can ask your host for a knife and fork, though you should definitely try to use chopsticks. Even if you fumble with them, your host will understand. But if you do not try at all, your host could take offense.

How to Use Chopsticks

- Chinese chopsticks are usually longer than Japanese chopsticks, and blunt-ended rather than pointed. When you are dining in Asia, you may not be offered any Western utensils, so be sure to practice using chopsticks before you go.

- The chopsticks rest in the curvature between your thumb and index finger and are steadied against the ring finger. Hold the chopsticks about two-thirds of the way up. Keep the tips pointed downward toward the table.
- The upper stick is held by your thumb, index, and middle fingers. The lower stick is held stationary while the upper stick moves to create a pinching effect.
- If you lose your grip on your chopsticks by holding them too tightly or too far down, gently tap them on the table to realign your grip.
- When you wish to put your chopsticks down, place them on the rest provided or on top of your plate.

Tips on Chopsticks Etiquette

- Use serving chopsticks if they are provided. If not, turn your chopsticks around and use the gripping end to pick up food from the platter.
- Do not stand your chopsticks in a vertical position in your bowl—this is considered inauspicious as it looks like sticks of incense in a bowl of ashes, which is used at funerals.
- Do not cross paths with your neighbor's chopsticks when you reach for food.
- Do not take food using another person's chopsticks.
- Do not gesture or point with your chopsticks.
- Do not spear food with your chopsticks
- Do not lick your chopsticks.

WINING AND TOASTING

Wining and toasting are the sine qua non of Chinese meals and banquets. As in the West, when drinks start to flow, people usually become more relaxed and conversations come easily. In particular, toasting is an acknowledgement of the friendship and business relationship forged between you and your partners. Hence, expect a series of toasts and a fair bit of drinking, even if you are a woman.

Drinking in China

"The Chinese like to toast many, many times. While drinking and toasting has been reduced quite a bit, it is still expected, and so I do it to be polite. Besides, it is fun. I see a lot less drinking today and often [the hosts] will serve tea or soda. There is a movement to be healthier, so [the Chinese] do less drinking and smoking. You can also say, 'I am watching my health,' and order a soda. It is a polite way to decline drinking." (Austin, Texas)

During the dinner, toasting can be made either to all participants by the host, to an entire table, or between two participants at a table. The host will initiate the first toast, usually after making an introductory speech. The guest of honor then returns the toast. During the dinner, everyone will continue to toast each other. Women who are guests of honor should initiate or return a toast as required. Do not defer to your male colleagues.

When toasting, hold your cup in both hands. To accept a toast, smile, raise your glass, make eye contact, return a few kind words to your host, and if are up to the task, down your drink in one swallow. This is known as *ganbei* (downing your cup), and in China, it is considered giving face to your host when you do so. Toasts may be conducted sitting or standing. At all times, follow your host's lead.

At Chinese dinners, it is the responsibility of the host rather than the waiters to see that the guests' drinking glasses are kept filled. If you do not wish to have your glass refilled, keep it full so that no more is poured. But this will likely be hard if you keep getting toasted or toast others.

Women too are expected to participate in some drinking, although some report that there is less drinking today. It will depend on your host and where you are in China. As a woman, if you drink very well, that would actually impress your hosts. However, it is possible for foreign women to feign or confess illness or weak drinking capacity. In such instances, you can sip your wine glass instead of downing it or toast with tea instead of wine. If you know you can't drink, you should try to bring a few colleagues who can drink on your behalf.

CHINESE BANQUETS

At a Chinese-style banquet, guests are usually seated at a round table, with the key guest, such as the team leader, traditionally seated in the most northern position to the left of the host. (In ancient days, people carried their swords in their right hands. The host demonstrated his trust and goodwill by seating the chief guest on the left, which gave the guest an advantage should a fast-draw sword fight ensue.) These days, not everyone observes traditional protocol, so in all cases, you should follow the lead of your host. Chinese hosts will often accompany each guest to the door when a meal or party ends. High-ranking guests may be accompanied to their cars and the host will wait until they drive away before leaving.

- Banquets are celebration feasts that last about two to three hours and are larger and more formal than business dinners.
- If you are invited to a formal banquet, it is important to arrive at the restaurant on time, though they usually do not start on time.
- If you are the guest of honor at a formal banquet, you will sit to the left of the host.
- Cocktails are not served before dinners or banquets, but tea or soda is served before all the guests are seated.

- When everyone is seated and the banquet is ready to begin, the host will make a brief congratulatory speech and offer a welcoming toast. He or she will then initiate the meal and make a symbolic serving to the guest of honor.
- Have some complimentary remarks prepared so you can respond appropriately, usually at the end of the banquet.
- If you are the guest of honor, you are expected to be the first to sample any dish that is served. If you see people waiting, start eating.
- After the meal, the guest of honor should be the first to leave.

Wedding banquets are probably the most common type of banquet in China. You might be invited to attend one if you develop friendships with your Chinese counterparts. At wedding banquets, guests usually offer red paper envelopes (*hongbao*) of cash to the bride and groom as a gift and blessing to the couple. For more on Chinese weddings, see "Chinese Wedding Traditions," www.chcp.org/wedding.html.

More Tips on Dining

Before the Meal

- If your Chinese associates invite you to a meal, your host will be the one ordering the food. If you have dietary restrictions (vegetarian, seafood allergies, etc.), advise your host beforehand, so that he or she will have ample time to order accordingly.
- If you are the highest in rank or the focal member of the meeting, you will be invited to sit next to the host during the dinner.

- If you are the one hosting the meal, you will do the ordering. You may get a menu designed for visiting Westerners rather than for locals, but you can ask the waiter or your host to help you order authentic Chinese food. Have them advise you on which items are fresh for that day, what to order, how many items, etc.

- Because food is shared, do not order one dish just for yourself. Order one dish per person in the group, including an appetizer, soup, and a dessert (usually fruit).

- Keep the *yin* and *yang* principles in mind when making your choices (see "Principles of Chinese Quisine," below.)

During the Meal

- Do not reach across the table; wait for the tray to be turned to you.

- Don't rummage through the serving dishes with your chopsticks to get the best morsels, but select the piece closest to you from the nearest dish.

- When you take food from a serving plate, don't put it straight into your mouth. Transfer it to your own plate first.

- To eat large pieces of food, raise the piece to your mouth with your chopsticks, bite off a small piece, and return it to your plate. You may prefer to use your chopsticks to break the large piece into smaller pieces first.

- If there are bones or shells in your food, leave them on a small side plate. If there is no side plate, leave them on the table.

- Your host, who is obliged to take care of you, may try continually to refill your plate and rice bowl. Politely refuse when you have had enough. You may have to refuse a few times before your refusal is finally accepted.

- When you serve yourself, don't take the last piece on the dish, as it will signal that you have not had enough.
- Leave some food on your plate to indicate that you've had enough. If not, the host will keep serving you.

Concluding the Meal

- The serving of the soup signals the end of the meal.
- When you've finished eating, lay your chopsticks neatly on the chopstick stand.
- As is traditional in Asia, your host may seem to apologize for a humble meal. In response, thank him or her for the wonderful food.
- At the end of the dinner, the guest of honor rises to graciously thank the host on everyone's behalf.
- Your host will likely go home after the meal. While the Chinese like to converse during dinner, they do not linger around the table for small talk. As one woman commented, "It is usually the Westerners who hang around after the dinner, while the Chinese just eat and run." For men, however, you might be invited to more drinks, a karaoke session, or the like.
- Before you leave the country, be sure to invite your hosts to your country and indicate your sincerity in reciprocating their treat. Don't provide a more expensive dinner than your hosts did, as this could embarrass them.

In short, do not feel intimidated by elaborate Chinese protocols for banquets. While it is helpful to know what the social norms are, the more important thing is to be polite and to demonstrate goodwill. If in doubt, follow Western etiquette. You do not have to apologize for your non-Chinese manners, but your guests will appreciate your knowledge of, or at least interest in, the way things are done in China.

Chinese Food and Beverage

> Rice affected by the weather or turned (a man) must not
> eat, nor fish that is not sound, nor meat that is high. He
> must not eat anything discolored or that smells bad. He
> must not eat what has been crookedly cut, or any dish
> that lacks its proper seasoning. The meat that he eats
> must at the very most not be enough to make his breath
> smell of meat rather than of rice. As regards wine, no
> limit is laid down; but he must not be disorderly.
>
> *The Analects of Confucius*

Food and eating are taken quite seriously in Asia. In fact, a standard greeting in Chinese, means "Have you eaten?" The idea is that if you have eaten, then you must be feeling fine. Chinese cuisine is measured in four aspects: *se* (color), *xiang* (fragrance), *wei* (taste), and *mei* (appearance). One distinctive aspect of Chinese cuisine is the attention given to how ingredients are cut before they are cooked and assembled. Often the aesthetic placement of food on a dish is more important than the size of the serving. What is perhaps least known in the West is that Chinese food is actually very diverse.

PRINCIPLES OF CHINESE CUISINE

The balancing of opposing factors, such as sun and moon, light and dark, male and female, called *yin* (feminine energy) and *yang* (masculine energy), is a central concept in Chinese philosophy and also in cooking. Applied to all areas of one's life, including food, it is thought to bring about and preserve harmony of body and mind. Daniel Reid, author of *The Tao of Health, Sex, and Longevity*, describes how an elaborate system of food pharmacology was developed in ancient China based on the cosmic theory of *yin* and *yang*, and the five elements of earth, air, fire, water, and metal. *Yang* foods are hot foods that stimulate the body. *Yin* foods are cool foods that calm the system. Neutral foods are a balance of the *yin* and the *yang*. For example, whole barley is a neutral food—the *yang* element heats up the body while the *yin* element cools the brain.

An ideal meal should be *yin-yang* balanced. For example, if you have a deep-fried (*yang*) dish, pair it with a steamed (*yin*) dish; if you order beef (*yang*), pair it with vegetable (*yin*). Variety is good; so avoid ordering more than one dish of the same type of meat or ingredient. If you are unsure, ask your host or waiter for the best combination of dishes to order.

REGIONAL CUISINES

Diverse styles of Chinese food originated in different regions of China. The four basic regional styles are: Southeastern (Guangzhou and Chaozhou), Northern (Beijing and Shandong), Eastern or Coastal (Shanghai), and Southwestern (Sichuan and Hunan). After these four come Fujian (also known as Hokkien) and Kejia (Hakka) from southern China.

Cantonese cuisine originates from the region around Guangzhou (or Canton) in the south of China. Since so many Cantonese established themselves early in Western countries, many of us in the U.S., Europe, and Australia associate Cantonese cuisine with Chinese cuisine in general. Cantonese style is characterized by enhancing the original flavor of each ingredient using a little seasoning. Common Cantonese dishes include wonton, shark fin's soup, mu shu pork, and barbeque pork. The typical Cantonese cuisine in America is dim sum, or small tidbits. At dim sum restaurants, waiters push carts to diners that are filled with a variety of steamed and fried dumplings as well as other dishes. Popular desserts include egg custard, fruit sago, and red bean pie.

Chiuchow cuisine originates from the city of Chaozhou in Guangdong Province. It is similar to Cantonese cooking and is well known for its seafood, vegetarian dishes, and rice soup. Other common dishes include steamed goose, cold crab, shrimp balls, and oyster pancakes. Chaozhou food is light, refined, and delicate. Many of the dishes are steamed, boiled, or stir-fried.

Shanghai cuisine features vegetables and noodles over rice flavored with soy sauce, fresh fish and seafood, especially shellfish, smoked fish, and drunken chicken (chicken cooked in wine). This is the style of Chinese food that many Americans say is on the oily side and rather heavy for their palates.

> *Dietary Restrictions*
> "The Chinese in the big cities are more aware of what Americans will eat and will not eat. For example, if you do not eat pork or shellfish, or you are a vegetarian, tell them about diet restrictions right away. If you are at a meal and you do not eat [their special dishes], it will be a loss of face to your hosts, as they will feel that they are not taking care of you." (Denver, Colorado)

Inland regions, which are hot and humid, use more spices and chili, which help to preserve food. Southwestern food is highly spiced, peppery, and oily. Sichuan and Hunan dishes are seasoned generously with chili peppers and garlic. Popular dishes include fragrant eggplant, frog legs, hot-and-sour soup, kung pao chicken, and twice-cooked pork. If you have a taste for spicy food, you should try the Sichuan hot pot, red-colored soup swirling with chili, in which meat and vegetables are cooked.

Beijing and Shandong cuisine is a blend of Mongolian and Manchurian cooking, which uses generous amounts of wine, garlic, and scallions. Northern cuisine is based on wheat rather than rice. Popular Western choices include noodles, pancakes, meat pies, soybean milk and curd. Peking duck, a particular favorite, is served in its crisp skin with scallions and a special plum sauce. Another delicacy is Tender Beggar's Chicken, which supposedly gets its name from the story of a beggar who stole a chicken from the emperor and hid it by burying it in the ground to cook it. The chicken is stuffed with herbs, onions, and Chinese cabbage, wrapped in lotus leaves, sealed in clay, and baked all day.

Fujian (or Hokkien) Province is on China's east coast and is known for its seafood and light soups. Some popular foods include suckling pig and egg rolls. Hakka cuisine originates from southeastern China, where fresh produce was hard to come by. The Hakka people relied upon dried and preserved ingredients such as fermented bean curd and onion. Common dishes include fried pork with fermented bean curd, duck stuffed with rice, and salt-baked chicken.

Hosting in Your Home Country

When your Chinese partners visit you in the West, you should plan to offer the same degree of hospitality they offered you in China. If you are the team leader, you should lead not only the business meetings, but also the social and dining events.

The Chinese will often include many people at business dinners as a sign of welcome and respect for their guests. When hosting them, it is a good idea to do the same. Learn in advance how many guests you will be hosting, and try to ensure a balance on your side by including other business colleagues. If you can, it is best to match title for title, rank for rank.

Apply the same logic of etiquette described earlier when in your country. As you are the host, be prepared to initiate the meal and the conversations. As always, keep the dinner conversation positive.

Make sure to take good care of your guests. The Chinese may make few requests; however, they generally expect their host to organize activities and to see to their needs. Accordingly, you should ask what their plans are, what they hope to do while they are visiting, and if there is anything special they want to accomplish before they leave, like visiting a renowned tourist attraction or shopping for souvenirs. If you have the time and inclination, try to socialize after office hours with your guests. It's a generous touch and will enhance your relationship. For example, a golf or tennis game, or a shopping or sightseeing trip, would be appreciated. Try to arrange one outing with them to show that you enjoy being with your guests. If you can't go along with them, provide a list of things to see, places to go, and restaurants to try, or better yet, arrange a sightseeing excursion for them. Your efforts will be appreciated and reciprocated.

> ### *Eager to Go*
> "You should stay until the last course of the dinner. I find that the Chinese are just as anxious if not more so to leave the dinner and go home. Sometimes they rush out faster than us!"
> (Atlanta, Georgia)

- If you are hosting a meal, learn your Chinese visitors' tastes and requirements beforehand. If they have been traveling for some time, they may yearn for home cuisine. If they are visiting for the first time, they may have a specific Western cuisine in mind they would like to try, perhaps one they can't get at home.

- If you are hosting a group, be sure to select a restaurant that can accommodate a large gathering, preferably in a quiet location. If you frequent a certain restaurant and establish a rapport with the manager there, you are more likely to receive quality service.

- Make your reservation as early as possible; reconfirm it the day before, reiterating your requirements to ensure that the location of the table and its setting are suitable.
- Don't skimp on the meal. Take your guests to a quality restaurant that has good service, a pleasant atmosphere, and a wide selection of dishes from which to choose.
- If your guests seem unsure about what to order from the menu, make some recommendations; they will be grateful for your advice.
- Ask your guests for their beverage preference so that you can assist them in ordering for the meal.
- Order last and be served last if you are the host. This will cue the waiter that you are hosting the meal.
- As host, it is your job to initiate the drinking and eating. You can make a toast, or pick up your fork and encourage your guests to enjoy the food.
- If the meal includes any shared dishes, begin passing them to your guests counterclockwise around the table.
- Have someone in the host group closest to the drinks refill them for your guests.
- Be prepared to start a conversation about local events, sports, or other current topics of interest. In China, the host generally initiates the conversation, so your guests may sit quietly waiting for you to start.
- Handle payment by setting up an account, arriving early, and arranging to pay by credit card, or by excusing yourself discreetly from the table to pay the tab. Avoid having to pick up the bill at the table or pay in view of your Chinese guests.
- If your guests bring coats, pay any coat-check fees for them.
- It is best to accompany your guests to the restaurant and make sure that they secure transportation after dinner. You may even have to offer a ride to get them comfortably all the way back to their hotel.

BUSINESS GIFTS
IN CHINA

While many Americans say thank you and write thank-you notes to express gratitude, in China appreciation is shown more tangibly through gifts and favors. Gift giving in China takes place throughout the development of a business relationship, oftentimes at an initial meeting and even after the closure of a business deal. Gift giving is part and parcel of the cultivation of *guanxi* (personal relations).

If you are planning to present gifts at a meeting, it is important that you understand basic gift-giving protocol. Not bringing a gift can cause an awkward situation, refusing a gift may be interpreted as an insult, and giving the wrong gift can be damaging to your image. Gifts should be business-related rather than personal items. If you do bring a gift, be careful not to give anything that could be construed as a bribe.

American businesswomen share their personal experiences and advice on giving gifts in China:

- *On the value of gifts:* "While choosing a gift for someone whom I'm working with, I try to anticipate what kind of gift will be liked and appreciated by that particular person. The gift should match that person's tastes. He or she should feel that the gift was specially chosen for him or her in mind. Gift giving in China is quite different from the U.S., where there is a twenty-five dollar limit for business gifts. In China, the price tag of the gift can vary, depending on your relationship with the other party and the rank of the recipient. For example, in the case of a junior executive, the gift can be in the range of ten to twenty dollars, while in case of a vice president, the gift can cost up to one hundred dollars. If you want to present something that looks professional, U.S. regional wines (such as those from Napa Valley) are a good option. Unique gifts from your home district also give you an opportunity to let the other party know a little more about your background."

- *Choose thoughtful gifts:* "I think what is most effective are thoughtful gifts. For example when I went to China last year, I had the opportunity to visit the Terra-cotta Warriors and Horses. I excitedly shared my experience with our Chinese hosts. The next time they came to the U.S., they presented me with a very fine replica of one of the soldiers. The one gift had so much more meaning than any other gift I have received. So I felt I wanted to return the same degree of thoughtfulness."

- *Holiday gifts:* "In China, presenting gifts is important on festive occasions such as Chinese New Year, Mid-Autumn Festival, National Day (October 1), and Labor Day (May 1). For example, on National Day, employers give presents to their employees to show their concern for them. During the Mid-Autumn Festival, the Chinese present moon cakes to their friends and business associates."

- *Favors and gifts:* "If you are in a position of power, you need to be very careful in deciding whether or not to accept a gift. If you accept a person's gift, he or she may ask you for a favor later on. If you decline a gift, this indicates that you are not interested in doling out favors. The concept of owing favors is popular in China."

Below are some general tips for giving gifts in China.

Choosing a Gift

- If you are visiting a company and are unsure how many gifts to bring, purchase items that can be shared by the office, such as boxes of candy or dried fruits from your home country.
- Especially around the Chinese New Year, shared food items are appreciated by company employees.
- Gifts with your company logo are a good choice. Bring items such as appointment books, paperweights, pen sets, key rings, business card holders, paper weights, and golf balls.
- Inscribed crystal bowls or vases make good corporate gifts to an entire team or corporate division.
- Prestigious brands of wines or whiskeys from your local area are welcomed by the Chinese.

Gifts to Avoid

- Do not give clocks and watches, since the pronunciation of "giving a clock" (*song zhong*) in Chinese sounds the same as "sending one off to a funeral." Such items are therefore considered extreme bad luck.

- Avoid items that cut, such as letter openers or scissors, because they imply the severing of a relationship.
- Avoid food items, clothes, and generic products that can be easily purchased locally.
- Avoid handkerchiefs and straw sandals as they can signify the departure of someone or something.
- Avoid heavy gifts or breakables if your Chinese contacts will be traveling; such items would also be a burden for you to carry.
- Avoid giving flowers, personal items, or gifts for your counterpart's family members unless you know them very well.

Presenting a Gift

- If your gift is for a company, present it with both hands to the leader of the Chinese team.
- If you have a gift for each member of the team, present it to each person individually, along with some words of personal appreciation.
- Gifts may be given at the end of a visit or at the end of a dinner or meeting. If you see the gift giver the next day, thank him or her again.
- In a business setting, your gift will be received with both hands and then most likely put away to be opened later. The Chinese do not generally open or comment on gifts in public. You may later receive a verbal or written thank-you note.
- In China, it is customary to refuse a gift three times before finally accepting it, so you must continue to offer the gift

until it is accepted. However, be sure that the refusal is not genuine.

- If you are offered a gift, do not open it in front of your hosts, but wait until later when you are alone. Thank your guests in a humble manner.

Wrapping and Numbers

Be conscious of Chinese protocols for gift wrapping. A well-wrapped gift shows sincerity and thoughtfulness, while a sloppy job does not speak well of your image. It is best to wrap the gift after you enter the country, as customs officials may open your packages.

- Gifts wrapped in gold or red paper are considered auspicious. Red symbolizes happiness and gold means wealth.
- Neither blue nor white should be used for wrapping as these colors signify mourning.
- Pink, gold, and silver are also acceptable colors for gift wrapping. Avoid yellow paper with black writing as this is usually presented at funerals.
- Check regional variation on preferences for and taboos on colors. Alternatively, because colors can have so many different meanings, your safest option is to entrust the task of gift wrapping to a store or hotel that offers this service.
- Do not give flowers. In general, flowers are sent only for funerals or weddings.
- Eight is considered one of the luckiest numbers, as the pronunciation of "eight" *(ba)* sounds like "wealth" in Chinese. If you receive eight of any item, consider it a gesture of good will. Six is another lucky number that symbolizes blessings and smoothness.
- The number four is taboo because it means "death." Other

numbers to avoid include seventy-three, meaning "the funeral," and eighty-four, meaning "having accidents."

• In general, try to present gifts in even rather than odd numbers, for example, two pens rather than one.

Bear in mind, as one of the businesswomen I interviewed pointed out, that "what is different about China is that the *gifts are symbolic*, so you need to select them carefully. For example if you bring a bag of items, make sure it is not an odd number. If you give a set, make it a set of eight, which is a very lucky number. Also, do not show up with a very expensive gift that outdoes [your counterpart's] gift and causes an unintended loss of face." Interestingly, another engineer related that "even in product engineering, we have always left the number four out of our Chinese product development numbering system because it has such bad connotations." Being aware of the symbolic meanings behind numbers and gifts can help avoid embarrassment.

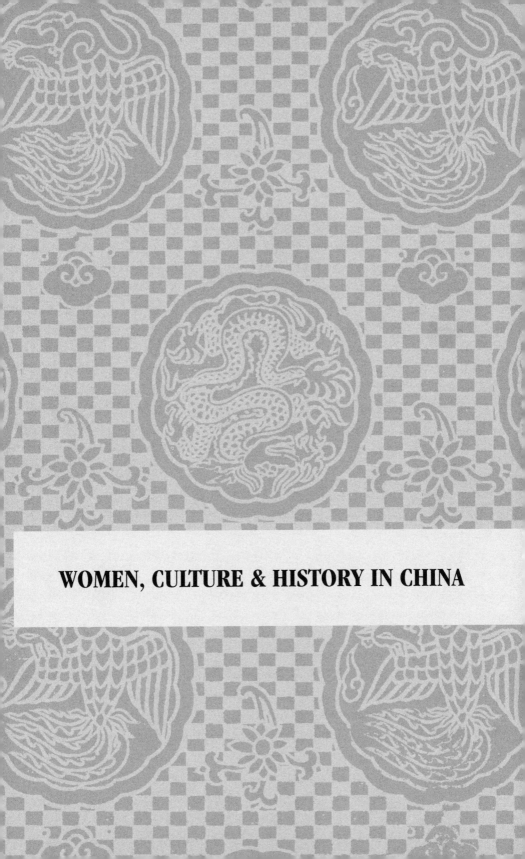

WOMEN, CULTURE & HISTORY IN CHINA

10

CHINESE WOMEN IN THE PAST

By Patricia D. Wilen, Ph.D.

"When a son is born,
Let him sleep on the bed,
Clothe him with fine clothes,
And give him jade to play . . .
When a daughter is born,
Let her sleep on the ground,
Wrap her in common wrappings,
And give broken tiles to play . . ."

Ancient Chinese "Book of Songs"

Women under Imperial Rule

China was a patriarchal society for centuries. Chinese families without sons feared poverty and neglect. The male offspring represented continuity of lineage and protection in old age.

During the second century B.C., Confucianism and its code of behavior became something of a state religion. Confucianism emphasized hierarchy, according to which each individual was defined by his or her role in society: as son, as daughter, husband, wife, mother, father, and so on. Citizens were subject to the will of the emperor, the son to the father, the wife to the husband. In childhood, a female was obedient to her father, then to her husband, and after her husband's death, to her sons.

Women represented the *yin*, or negative principle, and men the *yang*, or positive principle. While *yin* and *yang* are complementary elements meant to be in balance, *yang* (men) long dominated over *yin* (women).

Prior to 1950 women in China worked at home, where they were responsible for household chores, raising livestock, weaving, and various other supplementary jobs. Women were largely uneducated, with the emphasis placed on being an obedient wife and a good mother. A woman was expected to be quiet, modest, tidy, and industrious, and to produce as many sons as possible. When she married, the young wife went to live with her husband's family. She was subject not only to the whims of her husband, who could legally take many wives, but also to that of her mother-in-law. Rural girls were often sold by their family to city factories or brothels. There were no legal protections for women.

Women under Communist Rule

When the People's Republic of China was established in 1949 by Mao Zedong and the Chinese Communist Party, Article 6 of the Basic Law pronounced that:

The People's Republic of China shall abolish the feudal

system which holds women in bondage. Women shall
enjoy equal rights with men in political, economic,
cultural, educational, and social life. Freedom of marriage
for men and women shall be put into effect.

In 1949, the illiteracy rate among women was 90 percent
and only 7 percent of women were employed.[32] The Chinese
Communist Party sought to emancipate and empower women, as
feudal domination of men over women came under heated ideo-
logical attack. The Chinese government adopted two of the most
important pieces of legislation in 1950: the Marriage Law and
the Land Law. Prostitution, arranged marriage, child betrothal,
and concubinage were outlawed. Marriage was to be based on
love and mutual consent. Free marriage, free divorce, economic
independence, and other concepts that were alien to the majority
of the population became the official code of conduct.

Mao stated that it was necessary "to protect the interests of
women and place the greater part of the obligations and responsibilities . . . upon men."[33] Husbands were expected to share
domestic duties. Neighbors were alerted to scold wife beaters.
Brothels were closed and prostitutes were given six months' al-
lowance by their former owners. Mao insisted on equality between the sexes, famously stating that "women would hold up
half the sky." The government allowed either spouse to apply
for a divorce. Many women who were not happy about their
arranged marriage sought and were granted divorce. The divorce rate in China during the early 1950s was as high as 1.3
per 1,000 couples, and was said to represent the dissolution of
"feudal" marriages.[34]

Not only were there campaigns to implement the Marriage
Law, there were also campaigns to mobilize women to participate in the labor force in order to rebuild cities, develop the
economy, and restore social services. Recruitment involved the
relocation of large numbers of women from rural areas to the cit-

ies, from densely to scarcely populated areas, and from regions with a gender-neutral distribution of the labor force to areas with a concentration of female-oriented employment.[35] With the Land Reform, landless men and women obtained some property for the first time in their lives. Women's economic status began to change as they earned their own income.

Along with the establishment of the People's Republic of China, the ACWF (All-China Women's' Federation) was established to keep women informed about their rights.[36] Women entering the workforce were encouraged to go to school, hold jobs, run factories, and become local officials. Sexual harassment was considered anti-revolutionary and subject to penalty. However, according to CEDAW (Convention on the Elimination of All Forms of Discrimination against Women), "when women's interests come into conflict with those of the ruling party and the government, the ACWF cannot represent them."[37] Hence, the ACWF played a limited role in helping women express their grievances to the government.

Furthermore, although the official rights of women had been established, women who attempted to exercise their rights faced tough opposition from their husband's family. Implementation of the Marriage Law brought about strong and widespread resentment from men. Murders and suicides of women who sought to end their unhappy marriages reached such heights that the government decided to weaken the Marriage Law in 1953. Collective stability rather than individual freedom, particularly the freedom of women, was given priority. During the years that followed, stricter requirements had to be met for divorce to be granted. The government stressed the importance of harmonious family life. Campaigns were launched to encourage women to be socialist housewives and model mothers.[38] The emancipation of women from feudal domination seemed to have taken a few steps back.

Women During the Great Leap Forward

In 1958 Mao introduced the Great Leap Forward in an attempt to catch up economically with Western nations. During this time, women were once again persuaded to join the labor force, particularly in the fields vacated by men who had been transferred to male-oriented industrial occupations. Everyone was a lifelong member of a work unit (*danwei*). The work unit provided women with conditions favorable to participation in the work force, including equal pay for equal work, child care, health care, housing, education, and family planning services. Newly established institutions such as cafeterias, kindergartens, and nurseries mushroomed and were mostly staffed by women.[39] According to one source, "there were estimates that 4,980,000 nurseries and kindergartens and more than 3,600,000 dining-halls were set up in rural areas by 1959."[40] Women were encouraged to go to school, and by 1976 comprised 40 percent of enrollment in secondary schools.[41]

However, the Great Leap Forward resulted in the death of millions of Chinese from famine and starvation in the countryside. Famine disproportionately affected females, for if parents had to choose between food for their sons or daughters, the daughters lost out. At around this period, Mao introduced the one child per family doctrine to limit population growth. Since boys were more highly valued, baby girls were often drowned or smothered. Although Mao outlawed the practice of female infanticide in 1949, it continued on the sly.

Women During the Cultural Revolution

The Cultural Revolution was a time of great chaos, terror, and violence, especially in the major cities like Beijing. Even high-ranking officials were subject to political purges, where they would be publicly humiliated and beaten. Ironically, it was also at this time that gender equality progressed rapidly. Women's labor force participation remained high, and women's representation in higher education was higher during the Cultural Revolution than in earlier or later times.

However, as the bureaucratic apparatus began to crumble under political instability, the All Women's Federation was forcibly suspended. Wang Zheng, an American scholar of Chinese feminism, points out that the ultra-leftist Cultural Revolution Movement that lasted for ten years had completely ignored women's issues. Women were either barely differentiated from men or they were simply rendered masculine.[42] During the Cultural Revolution, men and women alike wore the same dull, unisex outfit, shouting slogans like, "Whatever men can do, women can do too!"

Women in the Reform Era

The reform movement that started at the end of the 1970s, following Deng Xiaoping's rise to power, brought phenomenal success to China's economy. In the reform era, to get rich is glorious. By 1997, private enterprise was formally recognized as an important element in the new market economy. State-owned industries dominated 70 percent of the market in 1978 but only 24 percent in 2000.[43] As women became more economically independent, they rose in status in their families and made more decisions regarding their children and their own needs. Women also took up leadership positions. By 1973 women made up 20 percent of the members of the Tenth National Party Congress.[44]

Unfortunately, as China becomes more capitalist, there has been a resurgence of the sexism that had been so vehemently criticized under Mao's socialist rule. In the new market economy, corporate profits rather than the welfare of workers is the primary goal. Up until the 1980s, women who worked in state-owned companies had generous maternity leave and child care, but these benefits have been cut back.

Unemployment has become a major concern since reform, especially for women. In a company downsizing or restructuring, women are the first to be laid off and the last to be hired. Women made up 43 percent of the labor force in 1982 and 38 percent in 1992. The *Workers Daily* reported that 60 percent of laid-off workers were women. In 1988, 80 percent of female university graduates sent by placement offices to job sites were rejected. In 1990, women earned 83 percent of men's pay, and by 1999, they earned only 70 percent.[45] In the drive for greater profits, businesses see maternity leave and child care as a financial burden, so avoid hiring women. Employers cite women's family responsibilities, especially to their children, as a major deterrent. Further, because of their family responsibilities, women are less likely to have time to upgrade their technical skills.

Missing Girls

After the Communists took power in 1949, Mao Zedong regarded China's huge population an asset. As Baculinao reports,

China's sex ratio remained stable and balanced in the '60s and '70s, with an annual birth rate of 3.7 percent. When the famine struck, Mao urged birth control. Then, as part of Deng's reform efforts in the early '80s, China established the One Child Policy to curb population growth. This policy resulted in the prevention of some three hundred million births. The current population is close to 1.3 billion. The ratio of boys to every one hundred girls has risen steadily, from 108.5 in the early 1980s, to 111 in 1990, 116 in 2000, and 120 at present.[46] The Chinese government has noted that gender imbalance is a serious concern.[47]

The abortion of female fetuses and infanticide was aided by the spread of cheap and portable ultrasound scanners in the 1980s. "Prenatal sex selection was probably the primary cause, if not the sole cause, for the continuous rise of the sex ratio at birth," said population expert Professor Chu Junhong.[48] Today China has an unusually low female population. It is estimated that there are at least thirty million missing women in China, and that about one-fifth of Chinese men will never marry. Here are some revealing facts summarized by Baculinao:

- In a 2002 survey conducted in a village in central China, more than 300 of 820 women had abortions, and more than a third of them admitted they were trying to select their baby's sex.
- According to a report by the International Planned Parenthood Federation, the vast majority of aborted fetuses, more than 70 percent, were female.
- A report by Zhang Qing, population researcher of the Chinese Academy of Social Sciences, said the gender imbalance is "statistically related to the high death rate of female babies, with the female death rate consistently higher than the male baby death rate." Only seven of China's twenty-nine provinces are within the world's average sex ratio. Zhang Qing's report cited eight "disaster

provinces," where there was one-third more boys than girls.

- In the last census in 2000, there were nearly nineteen million more boys than girls in the under-fifteen age group. "We have to act now or the problem will become very serious," said Peking University sociologist Professor Xia Xueluan. He cited the need to strengthen the social welfare system in the countryside in order to lessen the traditional preference for boys.

Ironically, women are once again seen as a marketable commodity. Because of the shortage of women of childbearing age, hoodlums have begun kidnapping rural women, luring them with jobs in the city, and then selling them to the highest bidders as brides or prostitutes. From 1989 to 1990, over ten thousand women and children were rescued by the police.[49] The CEDAW (Convention on the Elimination of All Forms of Discrimination against Women) has criticized the Chinese government for doing little to mobilize the public against the abuse of women. Further, they point out that the government fails to prosecute officials who ignore human trafficking or who may even profit from it.[50]

The vast army of males without female partners can pose a threat to China's stability, argue Valerie M. Hudson and Andrea M. Den Boer. In *Bare Branches: Security Implications of Asia's Surplus Male Population*, they cited two rebellions in disproportionately male-populated areas during the Qing Dynasty. According to their analysis, low-status young adult men with few chances of forming families of their own are "much more prone to attempt to improve their situation through violent and criminal behavior in a strategy of coalitional aggression."[51] The growing crime rate in China has been linked to the massive "floating" or transient population, eighty million of whom are low-status men and women.

11

CHINESE WOMEN TODAY

By Patricia D. Wilen, Ph.D.

Women and Family

From the time of their birth to their marriage, most Chinese women live in nuclear families. In the first two years after marriage, most of them live with their parents-in-law, who usually have the final authority in family matters. When the young couple leaves to form their own nuclear family, husband and wife have decision-making rights in different areas. The wife usually has more say in making day-to-day purchases while the husband has more influence over employment and housing decisions.

Family life in urban areas differs considerably from that in the rural areas. Where urban families are usually smaller, often composed only of the parents and children, some rural families still have three generations living under one roof (*sandai tong-*

146

tang). In an urban culture, where mobility is valued and land is not an issue, female talents are better utilized. "You can barely find a patriarchal family in the city now," says Li Yinhe, a leading family sociologist in China. "Sixty percent of Beijing families are nuclear, run by husband and wife. In Chinese tradition, you need a male heir to carry on the name. You bear children until there is a son; it is extremely important for identity. Yet now 50 percent have no son because of China's one child policy and many don't worry about it."[52]

Once married, some 60 to 70 percent of couples no longer live with their parents—a big change. Since both husband and wife work, they often try to live just a few blocks away from the grandparents, who can take care of the children. Otherwise the children are placed in day-care centers or boarding schools. Sometimes couples are forced to split up if their jobs are not close together. Husband and wife may see each other only rarely. Despite such problems, family life for most people in the cities is stable, and family ties continue to play a major role in the lives of both parents and children.[53]

China's Strong Women (*Nuqiangren*)

Chinese women today enjoy more lifestyle choices, financial independence, and exposure to Western ideas. However women continue to bear the primary responsibility for rearing children and doing housework. Working and caring for a family is not easy without support from grandparents. Putting career before family is acceptable behavior for men, but not so for women.

There is a phrase in Chinese, *nuqiangren*, for describing strong or capable women. Discrimination and prejudice against "strong women" is deeply rooted in China, an outgrowth of its long feudal history. Young educated women have higher expectations and want to marry men who are well educated and successful. However, men prefer wives who are willing to stay home in traditional roles. Successful professional men have no trouble finding a mate. But successful women have a more difficult time. Philip Pan related that university professors often advise their female students to get married before they go to graduate school so they do not become overqualified for marriage.[54] Ren Ting, director of one of Beijing's largest matchmaking services says, "Everyone knows that *nuqiangren* have unhappy family lives."[55]

Whither Women's Status?

The change in women's status over the last fifty years, measured in terms of income, occupation, and education, has been inconsistent. As a planned economy has given way to capitalism in recent times, China has become a man's world again. After decades of advancement in women's rights (*nuquan*), women's participation in politics, business, and education is falling.

A pyramid structure exists in most organizations that is a throwback to the old Confucian hierarchy. The higher up the pyramid, the fewer the women. In the National People's Congress in 2002, the percentage of women in the 198-member Central Committee dropped to 2.5 percent, an all-time low in the party's history, from a high of 10 percent in 1973.[56]

One of many reasons cited for the decline in women's political participation is the weakening of "affirmative action" by the Party. During the revolutionary years in the 1950s, many women leaders emerged, such as Song Qingling (Mrs. Sun Zhongshang) as president of the People's Republic); Deng

Yingchao (Mrs. Zhou Enlai) as chairwoman of the People's Political Consultative Conference, and Madame Chen Muhua as vice premier. Today, the top political positions are almost reserved exclusively for men, with the notable exception of Vice Premier Wu Yi. As Leitner reports, competitive pressures of the new market economy have brought out gender biases that had been suppressed during the collective era.[57]

When given responsibilities, women are often expected to fill roles in "feminine" domains like education, health, and science—areas that require spending money, not generating it. They are rarely in charge of economic policies, which is a major portfolio for promotion. Women are further disadvantaged since they are required to retire at fifty-five years of age, whereas men retire at sixty or older. As top appointments are commonly made when candidates are in their late forties or early fifties, women are passed over. Thus women in China are underrepresented in the most desirable positions, such as managers and heads of the Party and government.[58]

Furthermore, in the private sector, women are also bearing the brunt of reform. In Tianjin, for example, women comprise 42 percent of the workforce but suffer 62 percent of the layoffs, due to the majority of women working in low-level manufacturing jobs rather than in management.[59] In business enterprises, only 1 percent of female employees but 7 percent of the male employees were in managerial and executive positions in 1988. In urban employment as a whole, about 5 percent of female employees and 13 percent of male employees were in managerial and governmental official positions.[60]

One of the major reasons for the lower employment rate of women in recent years is open discrimination against women, especially older women, by businesses and companies. Although discrimination on the basis of gender is technically illegal, the government does not seem to have much control over the hiring and layoff practices of private businesses. Although the Chinese government has laws protecting women's rights, human rights organizations claim that women's rights are often ignored in the interests of social harmony and foreign investment. As Deng Li, deputy director of the government run All-China Women's Federation, comments, "For many women, their lives are going backward, because the rules to protect them are no longer followed." [61]

The All-China Women's Federation

The All-China Women's Federation, established in 1949 when the Communist Party came to power, has been criticized in recent years for failing to help women. Critics note that its approach to empowering women is mainly to improve their productive capability and not to develop their interests. Thus many of its local branches focus on job training for blue-collar workers, neglecting entrepreneurs, college students, and other women trying to climb the rungs of power. [62]

"Often at the local level they will be training women to work as domestic servants," said Nick Young, editor of *China Development Brief* and an expert on social development in China. "That's a bit weird. . . . The Women's Federation is very hostile to women organizing independently." [63] Many of the ACWF's top officials see their primary task as supporting Communist Party rule. That could mean blocking the development of an independent women's movement. Women leaders in the ACWF are often promoted simply because they're women. However, "just because you're a woman doesn't mean you understand what problems women face in politics," said Sarah Cook, Governance Program Officer at the Ford Foundation's China office. [64]

There are few avenues for redress of gender discrimination in China, claims *The Convention on the Elimination of All Forms of Discrimination against Women* (CEDAW), issued by the United Nations Social and Economic Council. In fact CEDAW charges that the Chinese government blames women for facing discrimination by implying that it is their lack of self-respect, self-confidence, and self-reliance that deters employers. The government makes little effort to reeducate men on harassment issues or to protect women by giving them the right to take legal action.

Challenges for Young Chinese Women

Young Chinese women today face economic realities not faced by their mothers. They are part of the first generation who must find their own jobs. Since employment and welfare are no longer guaranteed, women find it more difficult to get jobs and easier to lose them. Gender discrimination is rampant. Male personnel directors readily admit that they discriminate against female applicants because they fear women will get married and become pregnant.[65] Many young Chinese women feel considerable anxiety, and many parents, bewildered by the rapid changes, have little advice for their daughters.

Fewer women are enrolled in higher education, in part because some universities openly discriminate against female students, acknowledging that they will choose boys over girls with similar qualifications and entrance examination scores. For example, in 1982 and 1988 respectively, women accounted for only 16.5 percent of students at Qinghua University and 20 percent at Beijing University, two of the most prestigious higher educational institutions in China.[66] Gender quotas for female admits have been much lower than those for men. Part of the excuse for institutional discrimination in higher education is the claim that women's marketability after graduation is not as promising as men's.

Another cultural and social factor that has contributed to women's lower educational status is the traditional belief that "it is a virtue for women not to be talented." This belief remains ingrained, leading many Chinese women to feel less capable and intelligent than men. Even college-educated women suffer from a deeply rooted inferiority complex. They are concerned about how they will be able to juggle a career with the responsibilities of wife and mother.[67] Roughly three hundred thousand women committed suicide in China in 2000, a symptom of the intense pressures that Chinese women face.[68]

Many young women, often from outside the city, have chosen to become "small wives" to wealthy businessmen. Extramarital relations have skyrocketed. The Chinese legislature has even debated criminalizing the taking of mistresses, a growing phenomenon. Another profound change in society is a surge in the rate of divorce, up more than 13 percent over the past two decades and usually initiated by women.[69] For centuries, ordinary Chinese have greeted each other on the street with "*Chi le ma?*" or "Have you eaten?" Now a popular joke in Beijing goes that people say "*Li le ma?*" or, "Have you divorced?"

Despite many problems, there are some bright spots, the most significant of which is the development of programs and scholarships on women's studies. The Center for Women's Studies in China was established at Zhengzhou University in Henan Province in 1987.[70] More have sprung up throughout the country. As Wang reports, scholars have engaged in the analysis and discourse of women's issues without government surveillance, which is unprecedented in China's modern history.[71]

12

WOMEN IN GREATER CHINA

By Patricia D. Wilen, Ph.D.

Doing business in Greater China means doing business not only in the People's Republic of China (PRC), but also in Hong Kong and Taiwan. While these three regions share a similar history, culture, and written language, there are also major differences among them: most notably, China remains controlled by the Communist Party, Hong Kong underwent colonization, and Taiwan is a vibrant democracy.

Political and Economic Background

HONG KONG

Under British rule for one hundred and fifty years, Hong Kong was exposed to Western cultural values and business models. Businessmen in Hong Kong are very competitive and sophisticated. The Hong Kong businessman is "unique, go-getting and highly competitive . . . quick-thinking and flexible . . . wears Western clothes, speaks English or expects his children to do so, drinks Western alcohol, has sophisticated tastes in cars and household gadgetry, and expects life to provide a constant stream of excitement and new openings."[72]

Hong Kong was reunited with China in 1997. Old ethnic and cultural ties have been revisited. Hong Kong served as an intermediary between the PRC and the Western developed world for many years. The people of Hong Kong and the people of Guangdong Province shared a common dialect and family connections, which are very important in doing business. As cheap land opened up in China, many of Hong Kong's factories moved there. Within twenty years Shenzhen, the closest Chinese city from Hong Kong, transformed from an agrarian economy to a manufacturing hub.[73]

Differences, however, remain in currency, laws, education, and even in the official language. Hong Kongers speak Cantonese, while most Chinese speak Mandarin. Hong Kong has a more transparent political system and a liberal market economy, while China is a one-party dictatorship. The people of Hong Kong have become increasingly vocal in their demands for more democracy. There have been massive demonstrations in Hong Kong against Beijing's repressive measures toward the local press.[74]

TAIWAN

Taiwan has a colorful and multicultural past but a troubled relationship with mainland China. Taiwan (or Formosa, which means Beautiful Island) had been occupied by the Dutch East India Company, then by Japan following the Sino-Japanese War, and was returned to China after World War II. Founding president Chiang Kai-Shek defected to the island with his troops after defeat by the Chinese Communist Party.

The Nationalist Chinese Kuomintang (KMT), led by Chiang, was repressive and corrupt. Over thirty thousand indigenous Taiwanese died in a massacre on February 28, 1947, known as the 228 Incident. During the "White Terror," thousands more dissidents were killed and imprisoned, leaving the Taiwanese with bitter feelings toward the Mainland Chinese to this day. After this initial stage of repression, however, the KMT began to administer the island. By promoting foreign investment and small and medium business enterprises, Taiwan soon became an industrial success.

Until the early 1970s, the UN and Western nations recognized the Republic of China (or Taiwan) as the legitimate government of China. However, in 1971 and 1979 respectively, the UN and U.S. recognized the PRC (or China) as the formal authority of China. Taiwan conducted its first presidential election in 1996. In 2000, the KMT was defeated for the first time by the DDP (Democratic Progressive Party). President Chen Shui-bian, leader of the DPP, promotes a platform of Taiwanese independence. This has brought much anxiety to the leadership in China, which insists on reunification, and also to the United States, sandwiched between the two.

Taiwan has a ban on direct trade with the PRC; fines are levied on companies that break this law, so all trade is routed through Hong Kong. Cross-strait trade is growing with Taiwan at a surplus of $28.3 billion in 2004. China welcomes Taiwanese businessmen and promises to protect their interests in the hopes of having them support reunification. In the meantime, the ruling pro-independence party has refused to facilitate cross-strait business.[75]

Differences between China and Taiwan are many and sensitive. Dr. George Lee, former Director of San Francisco State University's U.S.–China Business Institute, cautions that when you are in Taiwan you should refer to the nation as the Republic of China or Taiwan, but when you are in the PRC, always refer to Taiwan as the Taiwan Authorities. Economically, Taiwan has a per capita income of $15,000, second to Hong Kong at $25,000, compared to the PRC with a per capita income of $800.[76] However, Dr. Farid Elasmawi points out that despite the differences within Greater China, the three countries are tied together by common Confucian ethics.[77] Dr. Elasmawi suggests applying basic principals of Confucian philosophy to your business dealings in the three cultures if you want to be successful.

Status of Women in Greater China

The PRC, Hong Kong, and Taiwan share a similar Confucian culture where women traditionally play a subordinate role. Mainland Chinese women achieved great strides in their emancipation during Communist rule, but faced gender discrimination in the new market economy. Similar challenges exist for women in Hong Kong and Taiwan.

HONG KONG

Despite one hundred and fifty years of British rule, the ethnic Chinese in Hong Kong maintain a strong cultural identity with the Confucian tradition of hierarchy. The male is the dominant breadwinner and the female the family caretaker. Chinese men are raised to be aggressive and independent and women to be social and dependent.

Working women tend to be found in service industries, which offer less advancement opportunities and lower salaries. Highly educated women in Hong Kong frequently take lower level management positions.[78] Women constituted 49.5 percent of the Hong Kong labor force in 1999 yet held only 25 percent of managerial, professional, and semiprofessional positions. In terms of the wage gap, women earn 69 percent less than men in fishery and agriculture, 46 percent less in labor, crafts, and operations, and 12.6 percent less in administration.[79] On the bright side, as Hong Kong's economy moves from manufacturing to service provision, women have been more successful in finding employment. More women are enrolled in education programs to upgrade their skills, particularly in computer and business administration.

TAIWAN

Urban women in Taiwan earned only 42 percent of men's pay in 1995. Why is that? Taiwanese women have more years of schooling than women on the Mainland, so we should expect higher labor force participation and a lower wage gap. Xin Meng points to a significant difference in social norms that impact women's participation in the labor market.[80] In Taiwan, women who do not stay home after having a baby tend to be considered neglectful. This is in contrast to women in China, who have long been viewed as unpatriotic if they fail to contribute to work and production. Xin Meng also points to higher gender discrimination in Taiwan against married women than in China. While 87 percent of single women in Taiwan work, married women's participation is only 42 percent.

What Other Women Say

Confucian gender stereotyping continues to play a significant role in limiting the opportunities for women in Greater China. These cultural stereotypes also influence women's self perception and attitudes. In all three areas of Greater China, women still lag behind men in social and economic achievement, despite rapid economic progress.

The persistence of gender inequality will also impact a foreign woman's business success. Here are what some other women have to say about the gender situation in China compared to other Asian countries:

- "If I had to choose, I would rather be a female doing business in China than in other Asian countries. Women in China are held in higher esteem than women in Japan, Thailand, and Korea where I have done business. In China a woman can be the matriarch of the company. In my role as an Engineering Head, I have met many women business leaders in China. It is common to see women in executive roles, especially in family run businesses. In other countries I have had to bring a male interpreter or assistant along to help bolster my status there. This is not necessary in China." (Research Triangle Park, North Carolina)

- "You would much rather be a female conducting business in China than Japan. From what I can see, there are more highly placed women. I think this goes back to Mao and the Cultural Revolution, when women held up half the sky. In the Chinese government, you will see more highly placed women than in Japan." (Orlando, Florida)

- "I think China is one of the few Asian countries that has more equality for women in the business world. I feel it is more difficult for women in South Korea and Japan than in China. I think in all Asian countries you are foreign first and a female second. In these three countries I do get respected but I feel it is more of just being polite in Korea and Japan and not true business respect as I feel in China." (Mountain View, California)

# CONCLUSION

Final Thoughts

This book is written in 2006/2007, a time when China's progress is still accelerating and explosive. Each time I visit China I am amazed at the rapid development and changes that are occurring in the major cities, in their speed of construction and expansion and in the vigor of the business pace.

In 2007, it is hard to predict the future for China in terms of women, business, government, and global relationships. I anticipate that the Beijing Olympics in 2008 and the Shanghai World Expo in 2010 will accelerate opportunities, increase tourism, and create more awareness and perhaps increased synergies in business in this part of the world.

Unlike years ago when I conducted research for books such as *Doing Business with Japanese Men* and *Asia for Women in Business*, I have much more information at my fingertips to help keep apprised of what is happening globally. Daily there are thousands of articles, blogs, and rss feeds with updates and happenings from China in a variety of areas: new books, new business opportunities, corruption, Taiwan relationships, birth control, technology, women, and much more.

In today's modern environment it seems that global relationships can and will continue to become easier as technology enables more transparency. While this is true, the strong roots of culture continue to be passed on to each new generation, so we need to be respectful, informed, educated, and open-minded when working with other cultures.

My hope is that the concepts in this book will help businesswomen be successful when doing business in China, and that women will share their successes and strategies with each other so that continued progress is ensured.

Dr. Tracey Wilen-Daugenti

CHINESE HISTORY TIMELINE

200 B.C.

GENERAL

Confucianism becomes state religion or philosophy. Monarchies rule for centuries.

WOMEN

Women are subjugated. They have no property rights and no legal protection.

1911–1949   *Republic of China established*

GENERAL

Revolution to create the Republic of China is led by Sun Yat-Sen. Civil war and warlordism mark this period until Chiang Kai-Shek is forced out of the Mainland to Taiwan by the Chinese Communist Party.

WOMEN

During this time, China remains a patriarchal society. Women work at home and are mostly uneducated. Ninety percent of women are illiterate and hold low status in society and family.

The May Fourth Movement in 1919 begins to stir debates on women's rights. Feminist Movement and Women's Suffrage associations established.

1949   *People's Republic of China (PRC) established*

WOMEN

Article 6 of Basic Law established: "The People's Republic of China shall abolish the feudal system which holds women in bondage. Women shall enjoy equal rights with men in political, economic, cultural, educational, and social life. Freedom of marriage for men and women shall be put into effect."

All-China Women's Federation founded to keep women informed about their rights and to encourage women to hold jobs, run factories, and become local officials.

1950

WOMEN

PRC adopts the Marriage Law and the Land Law. Prostitution, arranged marriages, child marriages, and concubinage are outlawed. Large numbers of women are recruited to work in light industry in the cities. Education for women advances. Women are allowed to own property in their own name.

1953–1957   *First 5-Year Plan: Transition to Socialism*

GENERAL

Political and administrative centralization, nationalization of banking, industry, and trade. Collective farms established and private enterprises abolished. Communes are created and each person is assigned to a work unit (*danwei*).

1958–1960 *Great Leap Forward*

GENERAL

Man-made famine from forced industrialization kills millions of Chinese in the countryside.

WOMEN

Women are mobilized to participate in production and to work in newly created kindergartens, cafeterias, and nurseries. They receive equal pay for equal work.

1961–1965 *Readjustment and Recovery*

GENERAL

Production authority restored to factory managers. Communes reorganized. Secretary General Deng Xiaoping directs the Central Committee as Mao goes into semi-seclusion.

1966–1976 *Cultural Revolution*

GENERAL

Mao comes out of seclusion. Gang of Four led by Mao's wife, Jiang Qing, incites violent political purges throughout China. Major disruption to bureaucratic apparatus.

1972

GENERAL

U.S. President Nixon visits China.

1976

GENERAL

Both Mao Zedong and Zhou Enlai pass away.

1978

GENERAL

Deng Xiaoping reinstated as vice premier. Gang of Four arrested. Hua Guofeng assumes party leadership.

WOMEN

At this time women make up 20 percent of the Tenth National People's Congress. Ninety percent of women work in state-owned industries with maternity leave and child care. Women on average earn 85 percent of men's pay.

1979–1982 *The Four Modernizations*

GENERAL

Deng announces economic plan for the modernization of industry, agriculture, science and technology, and national defense. Economics rather than politics is in command. Decollectivization of farms. Formal diplomatic relations established between China and U.S.

WOMEN

One Child Policy established to control birth rate. Gender ratio of 108 boys to 100 girls.

1988–

GENERAL

Chiang Ching-kuo, Taiwan's leader dies, and Beijing calls for reunification.

1990–1999 *The Socialist Market Economy*

GENERAL

Economic reform gains momentum rapidly. Output and prices accelerate. Two thousand economic zones are set up to bring in foreign capital.

WOMEN

Ratio of 111 boys to 100 girls. Prenatal sex selection available along with cheap abortions. Kidnapping of women and girls on the rise as hoodlums sell them as brides or force them into prostitution. Average women's pay drops to 72 percent of male pay.

2000–2005

GENERAL

China is now the sixth-largest economy in the world. Only 24 percent of industry is government owned. Private enterprises growing from strength to strength.

WOMEN

Women compose only 42 percent of labor force but suffer 62 percent of layoffs. 80 percent of female university graduates sent to designated job sites are rejected. Women earn 70 percent of men's pay. Only 2.5 percent of women now serve in local government. Boys now outnumber girls 120 to 100. Growing crime is attributed to low-status males who have no chance of marriage.

★ INTERESTING FACTS ABOUT WOMEN IN CHINA

Women and Education

- More than two million children in China drop out of school each year. Seven out of ten children who drop out are girls.
- The "Spring Bud Program" has helped more than 40,000 poor girls in China's Inner Mongolia Autonomous Region continue studies.
- The Women's Federation in Inner Mongolia has received fifteen million yuan (two million U.S. dollars) in donations since the "Spring Bud Program" was launched in 1994.

Women and Career

- There were 1,263 academics in the Chinese Academy of Sciences and Engineering, but only 6.2 percent were women.
- In 2001, there were nearly 70,000 women at the associate professor level or above in China's colleges and universities, accounting for 30 percent of the total.
- In 2001, there were 730 million employees in China. Women accounted for 37 percent of the workforce in business, 25 percent in state departments, and 43 percent in services.

- More than half of China's women still believe that men should work outside of the home, while women are expected to stay within.
- More than half of Chinese female professionals choose to have a baby at about thirty years of age. "Baby versus career" is still a dilemma for professional Chinese women.

Women and Wealth

- A great variety of companies, from banks to PC makers, shopping malls to entertainment venues, are offering favorable services to take advantage of the rising purchasing power of women.
- From 1998 to 2002, women's federations at all levels issued a combined 950 million yuan in micro credit to poverty-stricken rural women. As a result, more than two million rural women shook off poverty.
- Seventy percent of Chinese professional women overspend. Professional women spend up to 39 percent of their income on shopping and beauty care.

Women and Marriage

- A Chinese woman spends an average of 3.67 hours on housework every day, 2.1 times that of her husband. More wives than husbands regard the division of labor as unfair.
- A survey revealed that only 2 percent of men complain that their wives are lazy, while 10 percent of women consider their husbands lazy.

- Since ancient times Chinese parents have given dowries to their daughters when they marry. Dowries nowadays include camcorders, air conditioners, mobile phones, computers, and cars.
- Many "only children" in China, spoiled by their parents, are shocked to find that marriage life is not as sweet as they had imagined.
- The Chinese legal system still does not consider it a crime for a husband to force his wife to have sex, reflecting the male-oriented bias in the law.
- By the age of thirty, only 1 percent of Chinese women remain unmarried, compared to 15 percent in Western developed nations.

Women and Sex

- An online survey jointly conducted by Sinanet and Fortnightly Chat of 2,910 women revealed that 60 percent of respondents experienced sexual harassment occasionally and 17 percent of them felt they were frequently harassed.
- Naked wedding photos are the hottest trend among young couples in once deeply conservative China.
- In 2004, 65 percent of women who had abortions were single.
- The gender ratio of AIDS victims has narrowed from 5 men to every 1 woman in the 1990s to 2 men for every 1 woman in 2005.
- According to the UN Population Fund report in 2003, 83 percent of Chinese women use contraceptives.

Women and Media

- Among 931 surveyed advertisements involving gender issues, 88 percent used women to promote products or as sex objects, according to a report released by China's Women Reporter Association.

- There is not a single major news topic in which women outnumber men as newsmakers. In stories on politics and government, only 14 percent of news subjects are women; and in economic and business news, only 20 percent.

- Women make the news not as figures of authority, but as celebrities or as ordinary people. Female newsmakers outnumber males in only two occupational categories: homemaker and student.

- Men are 83 percent of experts and 86 percent of spokespersons in the news. By contrast, women appear in personal capacities as eyewitnesses (30 percent) or as representatives of popular opinion (34 percent).

- For women, age has a crucial bearing on whether they appear in the news. Men go on making news well into their fifties and sixties. Nearly half of all male news subjects are aged fifty or over.

- In stories on crime, violence, or disaster, pictures of women are frequently employed for dramatic effect: 23 percent of women in contrast to 16 percent of men appear in related photographs.

- Female news subjects are more than three times as likely as males to be identified in terms of their family status: 17 percent of women are described as wife, daughter, mother; only 5 percent of men are described as husband, son, and father.

- News on gender equality is almost nonexistent. Only 4 percent of stories highlight equality issues, and they are in areas such as human rights, family relations, or women's activism.

- In ads, young and pretty women get many close-ups, appearing to flaunt their sex appeal as the camera zooms in on their face, hair, lips, and voluptuous figures.

NOTES

Introduction

[1] Antal, A. B. and Izraeli, D. N., "A global comparison of women in management: Women managers in their homelands and as expatriates." In *Women in Management: Trends, Issues and Challenges in Managerial Diversity*, ed. E. Fageson (Newbury Park, CA: Sage, 1993) 52–97.

[2] "Putting U.S. Businesswomen on the World Map with Trade Missions," http://www.enterprisingwomen.com/trade missions.htm.

[3] "One in 18 U.S. Women Is a Business Owner," http://www.roadandtravel.com/businessandcareer/careers/oneineighteen.htm.

[4] Xie Heng, *The Changing Role and Status of Women in China*. The 1990 Institute, 1990. http://www.1990institute.org/pubs/ISUPAP8.html. Note: Madame Xie Heng is a Council Member of the China Family Planning Association and of China's Foundation for Children and Youth. Before 1987, she served in China's diplomatic corps as head of special programs for women and family planning for the Chinese Embassy in London, as First Secretary in the Chinese Embassy in Washington, D.C. and as Consul of the Chinese Consulate General in San Francisco. Mme. Xie's husband is Ambassador Hu Dingyi, who served as China's Consul General in San Francisco from 1979 to 1983.

Chapter 1: Before You Go

[5] Michael Pennington, ed., *China Stock Directory*, 3rd ed. (China Economic Review, 2005). This publication is not available in U.S. stores but can be directly purchased from the publisher at http://www.chinaeconomicreview.com/shop/.

[6] "Online Chinese Tools," http://www.mandarintools.com.

[7] "Online Chinese Tools," http://www.mandarintools.com.

[8] "China National Tourist Office," http://cnto.org.

Chapter 3: Health Issues When Traveling

[9] Department of State Publication 10542 (April 1998). *Your Trip Abroad*. Retrieved July 31, 2005, from http://travel.state.gov/ Publications/yourtripabroad.html.

[10] American Airlines (n.d.), *Traveling While Pregnant*. Retrieved July 31, 2005, from http://www.aa.com/content/travelInformation/ specialAssistance/travelingWhilePregnant.

[11] Department of State, *Your Trip Abroad*.

[12] Embassy of the United States: Beijing, China (n.d.), *Living and Traveling in China*. Retrieved July 19, 2005, from Embassy of the United States Web site: http://beijing.usembassy.gov/medical_ information.html.

[13] Department of State, *Your Trip Abroad*.

Chapter 4: Business and Government in China

[14] Kenneth G. Lieberthal and David M. Lampton, eds., *Bureaucracy, Politics, and Decision Making in Post-Mao China* (Berkeley: University of California Press, 1992), 8.

[15] Michael Lampton, "Chinese Politics: The Bargaining Treadmill," *Issues and Studies*, March 1987, 11–41.

[16] Kenneth Lieberthal and Michel Oksenberg, *Policy Making in China: Leaders, Structures, and Processes* (Princeton: Princeton University Press, 1988), 3.

[17] Hengxue Huang, *Reform of China's Public Service Units* (*Zhongguo Shiye Guanli Tizhi Gaige Yanjiu*) (Beijing: University of Tsinghua Press, 1998).

[18] "China's FDI in 2005 Revised to 72.4 Billion," *China Daily*, June 8, 2006.

[19] Zhile Wang, *2002/2003 Report of Transnational Corporations' Investment in China* (Beijing: China Economic Press, 2003), 10–11.

Chapter 5: Doing Business in China

[20] Ming-Jer Chen, *Inside Chinese Business* (Boston: Harvard Business School Press, 2001).

Chapter 6: Negotiating in China

[21] Carolyn Blackman, *Negotiating China: Case Studies and Strategies* (St. Leonards, NSW: Allen and Unwin, 1997); Lucian W. Pye, *Chinese Commercial Negotiating Style* (Cambridge, MA: Oelgeschlager, Gunn & Hain, 1982); Nancy J. Adler, Richard Brahm, and John L. Graham, "Strategy Implementation: A Comparison of Face-to-Face Negotiations in the People's Republic of China and the United States," *Strategic Management Journal*, vol. 13, no. 6, 449–66; M. Deverge, "Negotiating with the Chinese," *Euro-Asia Business Review*, vol. 5, no. 1, 34–36.

[22] Lucian W. Pye, *Chinese Negotiating Style: Commercial Approaches and Cultural Principles* (Westport, CT: Quorum Books, 1992).

[23] Tony Fang, *Chinese Business Negotiating Style* (Thousand Oaks, CA: Sage Publications, 1998).

[24] Scott Seligman, *Dealing with the Chinese: A Practical Guide to Business Etiquette* (London: Mercury Books, 1990), 45.

[25] Pye, *Chinese Commercial Negotiating Style*, 89.

[26] Irene Y.M. Yeung and Rosalie L. Tung, "Achieving Business Success in Confucian Societies: The Importance of Guanxi (Connections)," *Organizational Dynamics*, vol. 25, no. 2 (1996), 54–65.

[27] Raymond Cohen, *Negotiating Across Cultures: International Communication in an Interdependent World* (Washington, D.C.: United States Institute of Peace Press, 1997).

[28] Tracey Wilen and Patricia Wilen, *Asia for Women on Business: Hong Kong, Taiwan, Singapore, and South Korea* (Berkeley: Stone Bridge Press, 1995).

Chapter 7: Gender Issues in Chinese Business

[29] "China to enact first anti-sexual harassment law," *People's Daily*, Dec. 30, 2005.

[30] See Rachael DeWoskin, *Foreign Babes in Beijing* (New York: W. W. Norton & Company, 2005).

[31] D. Mayer and A. Cava, "Ethics and the Gender Equality Dilemma for U.S. Multinationals," *Journal of Business Ethics*, vol. 12, no. 9 (1993), 701–8.

Chapter 10: Chinese Women in the Past

[32] "Structural Change and Economic Growth in China . . . Autonomous Regions and Municipalities 1949–1989" (Beijing: China Statistical Publishing House, 1990).

[33] Jonathan D. Spence, *The Search for Modern China* (New York: W. W. Norton & Co., 1990), 376.

[34] Judith Stacey, *Patriarchy and Socialistic Revolution in China* (Berkeley: University of California Press, 1983), 178.

[35] Yuhui Li, "Women's Movement & Change of Women's Status," *Journal of International Women's Studies*, 2001, vol. 11.

[36] Guo Hong, "Impacts of Economic Reform on Women in China," (Master's thesis, The University of Regina, Saskatchewan, Canada, 1997).

[37] CEDAW (Convention on the Elimination of All Forms of Discrimination against Women), "Report on Implementation of CEDAW in the PRC," Dec. 1, 1998.

[38] W. Scott Morton and Charlton M. Lewis, *China: Its History and Culture*, 4th ed., (New York: McGraw Hill, 2005), 274.

[39] Hong, "Impacts of Economic Reform."

[40] Stacey, *Patriarchy and Socialistic Revolution*, 214.

[41] Stacey, *Patriarchy and Socialistic Revolution*, 214.

[42] Wang Zheng, *Women in the Chinese Enlightenment: Oral and Textual Histories* (Berkeley: University of California Press, 1999).

[43] Morton and Lewis, *China: Its History and Culture*, 263.

[44] Heng, *Status of Women in China*.

[45] Hannah Beech, "The Sky Is Falling," *Asia Time Magazine*, June 21, 2003.

[46] Eric Baculinao, "China grapples with legacy of its missing girls," MSNBC transcript, Sept. 14, 2004.

[47] "Imbalance gender ratio a worry of China," *People's Daily* (English edition), July 1, 2004.

[48] Baculinao, "China grapples."

[49] Jessica Fulton, "Holding up Half the Heavens: The Effect of Communist Rule on China's Women" (history paper, Indiana University, South Bend, 2000).

[50] CEDAW, "CEDAW in the PRC."

[51] Valerie M. Hudson and Andrea M. Den Boer, *Bare Branches: The Security Implications of Asia's Surplus Male Population* (Cambridge, MA: The MIT Press, 2004).

[52] Robert Marquand, "Women in China Making Great Leap Forward," *Christian Science Monitor*, Dec. 17, 2004.

Chapter 11: Chinese Women Today

[53] Marquand, "Great Leap Forward."

[54] Philip Pan, "Thoroughly Modern Women Disconcert Many in China," *Washington Post*, Dec. 26, 2000: A20.

[55] Pan, "Thoroughly Modern Women."

[56] Heng, *Status of Women in China*.

[57] Kirstin Leitner, "Enabling a New Era of Change" (presented at the China Business Summit, Beijing, April 18–20, 2002). Note: Kirstin Leitner held a five-year term as the top UNDP official in China.

[58] Leitner, "Era of Change."

[59] Leitner, "Era of Change."

[60] Li, "Change of Women's Status."

[61] Beech, "The Sky Is Falling."

[62] Antonia Chao, author of *History of Cross-Straight Marriages*, quoted in "Taiwan-China: Love, Suspicion, Spy Charges," *Asia-Times* Online, April 9, 2004, http://www.atimes.com/atimes/China/FD09Ad04.html.

[63] Chao, "Taiwan-China."

[64] Chao, "Taiwan-China."

[65] Boye Lafayette DeMente, "Asian Business Code Words" in *Asian Business Strategy & Street Intelligence Ezi*ne at http://www.apmforum.

com/columns/boye.htm. Note: Boye Lafayette de Mente is a regular monthly columnist at the *Asian Business Strategy & Street Intelligence Ezine*. A noted author with over thirty years of experience in China, Japan, Korea, and other Asian countries, Boye's tips on doing business in the region are both pragmatic and enlightening.

[66] Beverly Hooper, "Gender and Education: China Education Problems, Policies and Prospects," in *Gender and Education*, ed. Irving Epstein (New York and London: Garland Publishing, 1991), 352–74.

[67] DeMente, "Asian Business Code Words."

[68] Li, "Change of Women's Status."

[69] Pan, "Thoroughly Modern Women."

[70] Zheng Wang, "Maoism, Feminism, and the UN Conference on Women: Women's Studies Research in Contemporary China," presented at the China Society for Women's Studies Conference, 1997. *Journal of Women's History*, vol. 8, no.4, 126–53.

[71] Wang, "Maoism." Note: Wang is also author of *Women in the Chinese Enlightenment: Oral and Textual Histories* (Berkeley: University of California Press, 1999).

Chapter 12: Women in Greater China

[72] Hugh Baker, "Life in the Cities: The Emergence of Hong Kong Man," *China Quarterly* (1995), 469–79.

[73], Michael Gallagher, "Shenzhen and Hong Kong: Links and Challenges" (paper presented at the American Planning Association, April 17, 2002).

[74] "Hong Kong's Defiance," *Time Asia*, June 7, 2004.

[75] Craig Meer, "The Politics of Cross-Strait Business," *Asia Times*, March 9, 2006.

[76] George Lee, *Doing Business in Greater China* (San Mateo, CA: Pioneer Publishing, 2001).

[77] Farid Elashmawi, "The Many Faces of Chinese Business Culture." Global Success, 2000. Note: Dr. Farid Elashmawi is a multicultural management consultant and negotiation consultant. He is the principal author of the book *Multicultural Management 2000*. Dr. Elashmawi has had many years of experience working with American, Japanese, and Asian organizations.

[78] Feinian Chen, Susan E. Short, and Barbara Entwisle, "The Impact of

Grandparental Proximity on Maternal Childcare" *Population Research and Policy Review*, vol. 19, no. 6 (2000), 571–90.

[79] Yun-Wing Sung, Junsen Zhang, and Chi-Shing Chan, "Gender Wage Differentials & Occupational Segregation in Hong Kong 1981–1996" *Pacific Economic Review*, vol. 6, no. 3 (2001), 345–59.

[80] Xin Meng, "Institutions and Culture: Women's Economic Position in Urban Areas of Mainland China and Taiwan" (dissertation, Dept. of Economics Research School of Pacific & Asian Studies, Australian National University, Canberra ACT, 2002).

SUGGESTED FURTHER READING

Current Reading

Dong, Jielin, ed. *China Business Laws and Regulations.* Saratoga, CA: Javvin Technologies, 2005.

Fishman, Ted C. *China, Inc.: How the Rise of the Next Superpower Challenges America and the World.* New York: Scribner, 2005.

Harvard Business Review. *Harvard Business Review on Doing Business in China.* Cambridge, MA: Harvard Business School Press, 2004.

McGregor, James. *One Billion Customers: Lessons from the Front Lines of Doing Business in China.* A Wall Street Journal Book. New York: Free Press, 2005.

Seligman, Scott D. *Chinese Business Etiquette: A Guide to Protocol, Manners, and Culture in the People's Republic of China.* New York: Warner Books, 1999.

Shenkar, Oded. *The Chinese Century: The Rising Chinese Economy and Its Impact on the Global Economy, the Balance of Power, and Your Job.* Upper Saddle River, NJ: Wharton School Publishing, 2004.

Xinran. *The Good Women of China.* London: Vintage, 2003.

Recommended References

Adler, N. J., and D. N. Izraeli, eds. *Competitive Frontiers: Women Managers in a Global Economy*. Cambridge, MA: Blackwell Publishers, 1994.

Antal, A. B., and D. N. Izraeli. "A global comparison of women in management: Women managers in their homelands and as expatriates." In *Women in Management: Trends, Issues, and Challenges in Managerial Diversity*. Edited by E. Fageson. Pp. 52–97. Newbury Park, CA: Sage Publications, 1993.

Cohen, Raymond. *Negotiating Across Cultures: International Communication in an Interdependent World*. Washington, D.C.: United States Institute of Peace Press, 1997.

Heng, Xie. *The Changing Role and Status of Women in China*. The 1990 Institute, 1990. http://www.1990institute.org/pubs/ISUPAP8.html.

Pye, Lucian W. *Chinese Negotiating Style: Commercial Approaches and Cultural Principles*. Westport, CT: Quorum Books, 1992.

———. *Chinese Commercial Negotiating Style*. Cambridge, MA: Oelgeschlager, Gunn, and Hain, 1982.

Seligman, Scott. *Dealing with the Chinese: A Practical Guide to Business Etiquette*. London: Mercury Books, 1990.

Wilen, Tracey. *International Business: A Basic Guide for Women*. Philadelphia: Xlibris, 2001.

———, and Patricia Wilen. *Asia for Women on Business: Hong Kong, Taiwan, Singapore, and South Korea*. Berkeley: Stone Bridge Press, 1995.

———, and Christalyn Brannen. *Doing Business with Japanese Men: A Woman's Handbook*. Berkeley: Stone Bridge Press, 1993.

★ ABOUT THE AUTHOR

Dr. Tracey Wilen-Daugenti
Managing Director, Internet Business Solutions Group, Cisco
Systems, Inc.

Tracey Wilen-Daugenti is the Higher Education lead for the Cisco Internet Business Solutions Group (IBSG). In her current role, she leads colleges and universities in innovation and excellence by using the Internet to achieve institutional goals. Before joining IBSG, Dr. Wilen-Daugenti held a number of positions at Cisco in the areas of business development, marketing, and operations. Prior to Cisco, Dr. Wilen-Daugenti held executive positions at Hewlett-Packard and Apple Computer.

Wilen-Daugenti was recognized in 1995 as a notable forthcoming modern academic researcher on women in international business. She has authored seven books. In addition, she has published numerous articles, chapters, and essays regarding international business. She is a frequent guest on national television and radio, an interview subject in news columns, and a speaker for key universities and business groups, addressing the topics of women, leadership, and international business.

Wilen-Daugenti holds an MBA and a doctorate in international business, and is currently a visiting scholar at Stanford University. She has been an adjunct professor for graduate and doctoral programs for a number of Bay Area universities. Her areas of expertise are international business, leadership, and women's studies. Dr. Wilen-Daugenti was recently named San Francisco Woman of the Year by the Women in Business Organization in San Francisco for her outreach in the fields of academia, women's research, and technology.

Wilen-Daugenti is the author of *Mexico for Women in Business*, *International Business: A Basic Guide for Women*, *Europe for Women in Business*, and coauthor of *Asia for Women in Business*, *Doing Business with Western Women: A Guide for Japanese Men*, and *Doing Business with Japanese Men*.

ABOUT THE CONTRIBUTORS

Yuen Yuen Ang
Ph.D. Candidate, Stanford University

Yuen Yuen is a Ph.D. candidate in Political Science at Stanford University. She studies Chinese political economy, including public finance and development of the services sector. She has also contributed to a forthcoming business guide to the ASEAN–China Free Trade Agreement (ACFTA).

Pamela Galley, RN

Pamela Galley, RN has over ten years of experience in health care. She is currently a Service Director at Kaiser Permanente. Pam holds a bachelor's degree in Organizational Leadership and entered the Master's degree program in Organizational Leardership at Chapman University in January 2007. She lives with her husband and two teenage children in Turlock, California.

Patricia D. Wilen, Ph.D.

Patricia Wilen, Ph.D., is a licensed psychologist and writer with a special interest in international gender issues. Before moving to the Bay Area, Dr. Wilen maintained a private practice in psychotherapy with a particular interest in women's issues. She served as consultant to the Center for Advertising Research in New York and as round-table moderator for magazines and research projects. She is the coauthor of *Asia for Women on Business*.

Dr. Wilen holds a Ph.D. in Psychology from Hofstra University, NY, and an MS and BA from City University of New York. She and her husband live in Pleasanton, California.

Other books of interest from Stone Bridge Press

China Fever
Fascination, Fear, and the World's Next Superpower

FRANK S. FANG

China is poised to be the world's next superpower, but are we really prepared for its dominant role? In engaging, accessible language, Frank S. Fang provides a unique insider's look at the fundamental "on the ground" issues faced by China and the West. Explaining key opportunities and conflicts embroiled in economic, political, and cultural relations, *China Fever* paves the way for understanding China's rapid acceleration onto the world stage. Frank S. Fang, an economist, is director of the Chicago-based Institutional Economics Center.

256 pp, 6 x 9", hardcover, ISBN 978-1-933330-55-6, $24.95

China Survival Guide
How to Avoid Travel Troubles and Mortifying Mishaps

LARRY AND QIN HERZBERG

Just in time for the Olympics in Beijing—the first humorous travel guide to China! Complete with survival tips on etiquette, resource lists, detailed guides to hotels, taxis, airports, and bathrooms, and first-person accounts of travel mishaps and info on how to avoid them. Veteran travelers Larry and Qin Herzberg are professors of Chinese language and culture at Calvin College in Michigan.

160 pp, 4 x 6", paper, 10 b/w photos and 1 map, ISBN 978-1-933330-51-8, $9.95

Business Passport to Japan
Revised and Updated Edition

SUE SHINOMIYA AND BRIAN SZEPKOUSKI

This updated guide offers a fresh, interactive approach to doing business in Japan, presenting practical tips in an easy-to-read format. It goes beyond the logistical details of meetings, courtesy, and protocol to uncover the thought processes and cultural values behind the behaviors and situations you will encounter—especially those that are changing as Japan's "blue suit" corporate culture gives way to a younger, laid-back, and more Internet-savvy workforce. Throughout you are encouraged to take the long view to develop lasting successes. Sue Shinomiya (Portland, Oregon) and Brian Szepkouski (NYC) are consultants with extensive experience working with Japan.

248 pp, 5 x 8", paper, 6 b/w illustrations, ISBN 978-1-933330-47-1, $14.95

Doing Business with Japanese Men
A Woman's Handbook

CHRISTALYN BRANNEN AND TRACEY WILEN

The only book to look at the *uniquely* delicate situation every Western businesswoman faces traveling to Japan or meeting Japanese clients at her home office. Using real-life anecdotes, cultural explanations, and extensive lists of tactics, it tells women how to quickly establish their authority and work effectively.

176 pp, 5½ x 8½", paper, ISBN 978-1-880656-04-4, $9.95